DIVIDED WE STAND

DIVIDED WE STAND

A Road Trip in Search of the Ties
That Bind Ordinary Americans
No Matter What

By Bill Newcott

Divided We Stand is a work of non-fiction. References to historical events were researched and depicted to the best of the author's ability. The descriptions of all individuals are done with the utmost respect by the author.

Published by Compass Rose Publishing
228 Park Ave. S #620056
New York, NY. 10003-1502

Hardcover ISBN: 979-8-9941958-2-6
Softcover ISBN: 979-8-9941958-3-3

First Edition

Author Photo by Carolyn Newcott.

To Carolyn

My Missing Piece

Table of Contents

Prologue: The Man in the Red Cap

The man in the red baseball cap is sitting at a sheltered picnic table, scraping at a wad of scrambled eggs flanked by two slices of crispy bacon on a cardboard plate. The mountains in the distance are rendered differing shades of gray by the sun, which rose two hours ago and is now almost directly in the man's eyes; still he has situated himself to take in the sweep of mountains, lake, and Martian-like desolation that typifies the landscape of Lake Mead National Recreation Area.

A short sidewalk leads to the shelter from the parking lot. I venture up the path, pretending to be intent on taking pictures. As I pass the table, I make believe I am just noticing his red cap emblazoned with the words "Make America Great Again."

It is two weeks to the day before Election Day 2024.

I nod in his direction.

"So, what are you hoping for?" I ask him.

He glances up from his eggs and gives me a toothy smile. He is a bit older than me. Probably mid-seventies.

"Son," he says, leading me to believe he might be blind, "I just want someone to save my country."

He doesn't seem ready to ask me to sit with him, so I stay where I am across the table, about five feet away.

"I'm worried about the country, too," I say. "I'm afraid we're heading for a split we won't be able to come back from. Everyone seems so angry."

"I'm not stupid," he says, as if I've somehow suggested he might be. It dawns on me that he's probably been called stupid, and just wants to get that part out of the way.

"I see what's happening," he says, and I can't tell if he's looking at me or past me, because his sunglasses are really dark. "The people coming in here, committing crimes, taking over towns. And the government just waves them in and pays them to be here."

I'm not surprised he brings this up. As the Presidential campaigns go down to the wire, immigration is a hotter-button issue than ever. And it seems also to be one of the most intractable for both sides.

I nod.

"I guess one way to look at it," I say, "is that we live in a country with so much opportunity, people will risk everything just to get one foot planted here."

We are just a few hundred miles from the Arizona/Mexico border: forbidding, sunbaked terrain not unlike the vista we're looking at right now. I cannot imagine taking my child by the hand and dragging her across that triple-digit hellscape on the chance I might find a job that will pay me three dollars an hour.

His gaze seems not to have shifted.

"Oh, I've got nothin' against those people coming in," he says. "Hell, my grandfather came here 'cause things were so shitty in Europe. But he did it legally, you see? I've got the papers."

He says those words with such immediacy I half expect him to produce those papers from his rear jeans pocket.

"What makes these people think they're so special?" he asks me without expecting an answer. "If you're not gonna enforce laws, why bother having laws? You think I could just drive down Main Street at 100 miles an hour and explain to the cop I was hungry?"

I still can't see the man in the red baseball cap's eyes, but I can tell he's giving me a "gotcha" look, even though I haven't exactly been arguing with him.

Still, I suggest, does he think everyone can agree that America is still the land of opportunity it always was; that we can all take pride in that and use that as our starting point of discussion? It seems like a more productive approach than focusing on the criminality of those crossing our borders illegally…or accusing those who worry about immigration as a bunch of racist isolationists.

The man in the red hat twists his mouth in a quizzical manner.

"These eggs cost four dollars a dozen," he says. "I don't know how much the bacon cost, but it wasn't cheap. I wonder if we can all agree that food is too damned expensive."

The light behind the man's sunglasses shifts a bit, and I can now tell he's kinda glaring at me. I'm here working on a travel piece about southern Nevada, and what kinds of things visitors could do if the Las Vegas Strip had never happened. But as our gazes scrape against each other, flint-like, the spark of a book idea flickers in the back of my brain. Impulsively, I share the notion with the man: What would it be like to see beyond the divisions in America, and instead look for the common denominators that link everyone here, no matter what their politics are?

"Well, I sure as hell don't want to be in any book," he says, but not in an unpleasant manner. "I think I just want to eat my breakfast now."

After taking a few token pictures of the view, I nod and say goodbye. I walk back to my car, past the man in the red baseball cap's pickup truck and travel trailer with Colorado plates. In the truck's passenger seat sits a woman, presumably his wife, and I can't help but wonder why he's out there contemplating nature and eating his eggs and bacon while she remains behind the windshield, staring straight ahead.

On the Boulder City radio station, a guy is reporting that one day last week, the temperature in this valley topped 100°F. The next day it was fifty. He marvels at the contrast.

I can't help but think about how, sometime in between, the temperature sat at a perfect seventy-two degrees.

***

Where is America's seventy-two-degree sweet spot? Does it have one? None? Many?

This wandering journalist has been crisscrossing America, examining its culture and history, interviewing Americans famous and not, for nearly fifty years. As I leave the man in the red cap in my rearview mirror, rolling toward Las Vegas across one of America's most desolate landscapes, I seriously consider if there may be value in taking one more such journey—this time not so much in search of a "story" as a sense of rediscovering the elusive truth that Americans are, despite their megaphone-toting differences, a single and singular people.

So, what if I were to make a grand circle around the country to determine the areas where Americans with differing perspectives still share core values and indelible humanity? Where can liberals and conservatives channel their passions toward a mutual humanitarian goal? The issue of abortion, for example, may generally be intractable, but both sides, in their own way, are arguing for the preservation of life.

The desert skirts by. My mind begins to scroll through issues that are famously divisive, yet possibly fertile ground for patchwork agreement. Guns offer one of America's sharpest divides, but don't people on both sides of that subject want, in the end, just to feel safe? Devotees of the Confederacy and descendants of enslaved people may read history through radically different lenses, but aren't they all simply seeking to honor their forebears? And might there also be a common path—even if it's as tenuous as a spindly sandstone arch—between liberal tree huggers and conservative land managers? Or between those who pride themselves on saying "Back the Blue" and those who eye police with suspicion?

And what about the man in the red cap? Sure, to him, images of undocumented people streaming across the border are scary and, maybe even infuriating. But isn't there some level at which he and even the most strident immigration proponents can agree that, even if they are here for just a short time, desperate people deserve some modicum of compassion?

Maybe. Or maybe not. In the end, I may well discover that Americans are irreconcilably divided on all those subjects. One thing is for sure: Until the sides put down their dukes and find ways to relate to each other, no one is going to be solving any problems to anyone else's satisfaction.

Who says Americans must be defined by their differences, anyway? Of course there are things that engender unity across the board. Music, for one: You can't tell me that the arenas full of faithful Bruce Springsteen, Taylor Swift, or Mannheim Steamroller fans are in any way ideologically homogenous. How about the arts more broadly? Is there a way to leverage their neutral ground into something decidedly positive? After all, devotees of Impressionism, both right and left, are equally likely to frequent the Dallas Museum of Art and New York's MOMA.

In truth, I have always resisted the notion of Left and Right. The term seems like an overly simplistic way to divide people, and it doesn't have a very noble history: The distinction was first coined at the dawn of the French Revolution, when National Assembly opponents of King Louis XVI sat to the left of the presiding officer and supporters of the crown sat to his right.

We all know how that turned out.

The drive back to town takes me from one incongruous feature after another: From the Palm-lined oasis of Rogers Spring to the sparkling artificiality of Lake Las Vegas to the seemingly unsustainable suburb of Henderson. By the time I arrive at Harry Reid International Airport, I've decided to give this project a whirl. I will fly home to Delaware, make a plan, and hit the road.

Maybe this is a classic middle-child project; launched by the kid with his arms outstretched between a warring pair of brothers. With any luck at all, I'll meet people who, despite seemingly unbridgeable political and social differences, have found ways to strike unlikely alliances without sacrificing their principles.

I'm not looking for a Kumbaya *can't-we-all-agree* moment. I'll settle for a lukewarm *we-are-not-that-different* respite.

It's a mission worth pursuing. It's a country worth saving.

Welcome Table's Steve Hammond

Arlington, Virginia: The Welcome Table

Descendants of Slavers and the Enslaved Hold Hands

My home these days (and for the rest of my life) is the Delaware beaches—for centuries a rural, remote farmland; in recent decades a gurgling melting pot of refugees from New York, Philadelphia, Washington, DC and their environs. But for more than twenty-five years, I worked and raised a family in DC—a town that can simultaneously instill chest-thumping pride in the miracle of representative Democracy…and heartbreaking despair from the economic and social inequities that persist in the richest country on the planet.

For me, those contradictions have manifested themselves for a lifetime. My parents were proud FDR Democrats, building a future on the foundations laid down by the New Deal. I can only imagine their mystification when, in 1960, their five-year-old son declared himself a supporter of Republican presidential candidate Richard Nixon.

I'm probably imagining it, but I can picture the two of them staring down at me as I calmly explained that because Nixon had stepped in to run the government while President Dwight D. Eisenhower recovered from a heart attack, RN was clearly more qualified than that JFK kid to serve as the Chief Executive.

But here's the thing: My mom and dad did not for one second try to convince me otherwise. I may have been a weird kid, but I was *their* weird kid. I grew up a left-leaning Republican in a proudly Democratic household, quietly hoping George McGovern would topple LBJ and silently celebrating Nixon's resurgence in 1968—a feat perhaps more startling than the once-defeated Donald Trump's return half a century later. On the other hand, as a high school student I realized almost immediately Watergate would rightfully dethrone Tricky Dick—who had, in any case, clearly lied about having a Vietnam peace plan.

Still, I remained a member of the Republican Party, which was awkward in college but served me well socially during my ten years in Florida, writing for *The National Enquirer* (which is another book entirely).

In 1990, I moved to Washington, DC to join the staff of *National Geographic* magazine. Being a Republican in Washington was simply part of the local landscape. (My neighbor was Lee Atwater, architect of the combative GOP ethos that reached its apex in Donald Trump.) But *voting* Republican in Washington, I soon discovered, was akin to rooting for the Big Bad Wolf while watching *The Three Little Pigs*. Not only were you going to lose every time; there was also an unspoken moral stigma attached to it. So, I lowered my head, kept my moderate (R) politics to myself, and went to work writing about pandas and space shuttles and Medieval London—and later, with *AARP the Magazine*, about movies and travel and Social Security.

Virtually every evening for those twenty-five years, I drove west on Constitution Avenue toward Virginia, past the White House, through the shadow of the Washington Monument. On dark winter evenings, beyond the Lincoln Memorial and across the Potomac in Arlington National Cemetery, the flicker of JFK's eternal flame danced below the illuminated façade of the Custis-Lee Mansion, the pre-Civil War home of Confederate General Robert E. Lee.

There is talk these days of erecting a triumphal arch between Lincoln and Lee, and despite whatever esthetic violations may result, it occurs to me that, thematically at least, it might not be such a bad idea: The improbable reunification of the North and South after the bitter bloodshed of the Civil War remains one of the great triumphs of the American story.

The Custis-Lee mansion is barely 120 miles due west of where I now live in Delaware. It occurred to me there could be no more appropriate spot to begin my journey in search of common ground than the site where postwar North and South were compelled to face each other—and come to terms with their enduring conflicts and aspirations.

***

The climb from the Arlington National Cemetery Visitors Center to Arlington House doesn't look all that challenging, but as I climb the steep incline, I realize the size of the hilltop Greek Revival mansion makes the onetime home of Robert E. Lee look a lot closer than it really is. Also, I soon discover, I can't walk straight up to the place, either—the paved roadway meanders among the thousands of headstones that mark the final resting places of military veterans dating back a century and a half.

Once I'm up there, though, even as a cooling Potomac River breeze kicks in, an enormous deodar cedar tree behind the house invites me to seek out a shady spot. The 150-year-old behemoth, more likely to be found growing in the Himalayas than in northern Virginia, flourishes here as the result of a post-Civil War beautification project.

I find a solitary seat in an array of wooden benches, lined up like pews facing the back side of the mansion. A shush of breeze wafts through the cedar's gnarly branches and, from somewhere in there, lurches the screech of a bluejay. A small knot of tourists begins to gather, and soon I am hearing the voice of a man who briefly relates the story of George Washington Parke Custis, who built the house, and Confederate General Robert E. Lee, who lived in it.

Still, the docent cautions, while Robert E. Lee is a chapter in the history of this house, "He's not the whole book."

And that is when he finally settles in on the story of the enslaved generations who sustained the property, inside and out, for the better part of a century: families like the Grays, and the Parks, and the Henrys.

And the Syphax family—the line from which the man speaking happens to be a descendant.

Presently, the group has to depart for a waiting tourist tram, and I introduce myself to the docent, Steve Hammond. I want to know more, and he is more than happy to oblige. It's clear he could talk about this place and the people who made it all day. It's also clear the story would never, ever get boring.

As Hammond relates the family histories of Arlington House—which entwine like the branches of that cedar above us—I notice he never veers off exclusively into the somber story of his enslaved ancestors. I sense he sees the history of Arlington House as a complex, multi-family saga both triumphant and tragic.

In fact, for that very reason Steve Hammond has for the past several years headed up a project to bring together descendants of both the Lees and their enslaved servants in a remarkable gesture of reconciliation and shared humanity.

***

Hammond has always been engrossed in the story of Arlington House, but his involvement became acute when, during the 2010s, the National Parks Service embarked on a years-long renovation of the place. Significantly, the agency wanted to be sure the renewed exhibits and signs would present an evenhanded and thoughtful approach to telling the story of a plot of land that, while now hallowed ground for America's military heroes, was once the site of a plantation that enslaved entire families.

For guidance in striking that delicate balance, the Parks Service turned to a Mississippi-based foundation called Welcome Table. Founder Susan Glisson—a long-time Civil Justice advocate whose portfolio includes reconciling Mississippi conservatives and liberals long enough to get a conviction in a forty-year-old Civil Rights murder—crisscrosses the country with her colleagues mediating in touchy local and national issues like Confederate statue removals and official apologies for long-ago lynchings.

The principle of Welcome Table—named after a traditional African American folk song—is simple, Glisson says.

"We don't try to directly resolve the issues that separate people," she tells me. "Instead, we simply place those people face-to-face and encourage them to share their stories and experiences."

The result, she says, can be life-changing.

"Eventually, we hope, the sides will come to know each other not as partisans, but as people."

***

To head the Arlington House project, Glisson turned to Hammond, a long-time earth scientist with the U.S. Geological Survey. In the convoluted manner that defined black family trees in the slavery era, Hammond's ancestor Mariah Carter Syphax was the daughter of an enslaved woman and white planter George Washington Parke Custis, the only grandson of Martha Washington.

Mariah asked her father for permission to marry Charles Syphax, an enslaved worker on the plantation. Not only did Custis agree, he allowed them to marry inside the Arlington mansion—and granted Mariah 17 acres of the sprawling estate. (Her white half-sister, Mary Custis, married Robert E. Lee, leading to the later designation of the house as the Custis-Lee Mansion.)

Because they were liberated before the Civil War, the Syphaxes became part of an elite African-American society that took hold in Washington, DC. Mariah and Charles had ten children who, along with their progeny, expanded their influence to become among the most important families in the country. The parade of significant Syphaxes included a founder of the first high school for African Americans, a major Philadelphia real estate developer, a prominent mathematician and dean of Howard University, a University of Michigan physician, a Tuskegee airman and the U.S. Congressman who led an attempt to impeach Ronald Reagan after the invasion of Grenada.

Hammond, then, was a natural to serve as a go-between in an effort to help members of the Lee and Syphax families find common ground. The Arlington House project was called "Finding Our Voice."

It was the time of COVID-19, but because the reopening of the mansion was already set, the groups couldn't wait until after the pandemic to meet. So, for two years, all those monthly sessions were virtual—with the participants still looking each other in the eye, just not in a circle.

"The first several meetings were kind of like arriving at a dance when you're a teenager," Hammond recalls. "We were trying to get people to step away from the wall; get them talking to each other."

Glisson took the role of moderator, prodding the participants to explore what it meant to be gathered together like this; and specifically, what it meant to be gathered, at least symbolically, in a place like Arlington House.

Predictably, while the Syphax descendants were almost universally enthusiastic about the project, those on the Lee side were more apprehensive.

"Some of them," Hammond tells me, "were self-conscious, thinking, 'Hey, what's going to happen here?' I mean, if you're a descendant of an enslaver, you're going to wonder 'What are those other people going to think of me?'"

For hours at a time, the discussions continued, even when they became increasingly uncomfortable. Slowly, the participants emerged from their protective shells.

"We built trust, with a capital T," Hammond says. "We built an ability to talk to one another, not as the descendants of slaves or enslavers, but just as people with a common mission." He explains that the process is not so much a matter of walking in another person's shoes as it is tracing the footsteps those shoes once trod.

"There are what I call 'blind spots' among people who are not living in each other's places," he tells me. "Everyone began to see how they are viewed by others, and to think a bit about how they view themselves. Most importantly, we began to hear each other in ways that enabled us to move on constructively."

Perhaps surprisingly, throughout the two-year process the Parks Service—which had summoned the families together in the first place—stayed totally out of it. The Welcome Table discussions remained completely private, without even regular reporting on their progress or lack of it.

By August 2021, the families had agreed on a list of ten items they jointly wanted to see incorporated into the re-opening of Arlington House to visitors. They invited not only representatives of Arlington House, but also of George Washington's Mount Vernon and the City of Alexandria—institutions with likewise difficult histories regarding slavers and the enslaved—to hear them out.

"They were charged with listening," Hammond recalls. "Just listen to what we had to say and what we wanted to try and accomplish, as a family circle."

Among the stated goals was to slightly reframe the narrative at Arlington House to make it more inclusive of everyone who lived and worked there.

"Right now," Hammon says, "the place is known as Arlington House: The Robert E. Lee Memorial. We want to have the site redesignated as Arlington House National Historic Site—to make clear it's not just about Robert E. Lee."

Importantly, the two sides made clear, they did not want to scrub away Lee, nor the remarkable details of his life and retirement.

"No," Hammond says, "it's about adding to the narrative—because there is a lot of history there that has, perhaps, not been fully told in the past."

An important part of that history is the unknown number of enslaved people who were buried there long before the place became a national cemetery.

"Many of my family, for example, were buried here," Hammond says, casting his gaze over the rolling hills of Arlington. "And they were exhumed and removed in the 1940s to make room for the military cemetery."

Today, those graves can be found at Lincoln Memorial Cemetery—a historically Black burial ground—in Suitland, Maryland, ten miles away.

Concrete results of the two families' convergence are ongoing. Walk through the front door of Arlington House, and you'll find a signed Letter of Commitment, drafted near the end of the initial Finding Our Voice process.

The two parties' aim, the letter states, is "to affirm the shared interests of the Park and descendant families in shaping and sharing how descendant family histories and legacies are presented to the public, how the national significance of Arlington House has changed and continues to change over time, and how management of Arlington House will be more accurate, inclusive, and holistic if based on collaboration between the Park and descendant families." The letter is signed by representatives of both families, along with the National Parks Service superintendent.

Today, new signs tell the story of enslaved families, and visitors can walk out back—beyond the spreading cypress tree—to experience the estate's former South slave quarters. Modest and whitewashed, the interior was recently furnished as it might have appeared in the days when the enslaved married couple Selina Norris and Thornton Gray lived there with their eight children: A rustic table, simple beds, primitive toy dolls.

On the other hand, legislation to rename the historic site, with 150 co-sponsors, has been introduced in the last three Congresses without passage.

Whatever additional interpretive signs ultimately get installed at Arlington House and whether or not the mansion's name will ever be changed are matters now out of the hands of the Lee and Syphax families. There's even a threat that all the new signage enhancing the story of Arlington House will be removed by bureaucrats who seek to soften the harsh realities of America's history.

But even that won't dull the lessons of Welcome Table: Connection and reconciliation are ends to themselves, planting seeds of shared humanity that will, with any luck, sprout and spread their roots throughout the forest floor of a civilized society.

For now, the most striking—and ultimately, perhaps, most lasting—outcome of the Arlington House/Welcome Table enterprise came on April 22, 2023, when some 100 members of the combined families walked up the hill at Arlington to convene on the grounds that, 170 years earlier, so inhumanely divided them.

Among them were Robert E. Lee the Fifth and his sister, Tracy Lee Crittenberger.

"Everybody was so gracious," Crittenberger told NPR. "No one cared what anyone's family had done in the past," she said. "All they wanted to know was, who they were right now? If this conversation can become a blueprint for other people," said Crittenberger, "that would be a whole separate victory."

Leah Coleman, an African American park ranger, echoed that sentiment: "Just seeing all of these people come together at this moment, at this site—it just symbolizes hope for me. If they can do it, we all can do it."

There was a time and place in this country, and not long ago or far away, when a black person merely touching a white person could have led to execution without trial. But on this spring afternoon, on grounds stained by tragedies told and still-secret, descendants of the slavers and enslaved stood in an enormous ring and held hands. Together, they sang "Lift Every Voice and Sing," the nineteenth century hymn now recognized as the black national anthem:

Out from the gloomy past
'til now we stand at last
Where the white gleam
of our bright star is cast.

There was that breeze again, wafting up the steep hill, whistling through grave markers and rustling trees that have shaded the entwined aftermath of Civil War and Civil Rights.

One more circle was closed.

Erik Angel

New York City: Laughing Through Their Fears

A multi-faith comedy troupe proves laughter is its own language

It's a sold-out Saturday night at Comic Strip Live, the oldest stand-up showcase in New York City, the place where Chris Rock stacked chairs in exchange for stage time; where George Carlin, Eddie Murphy and Robin Williams sharpened material before taking it on the road.

Pacing before the club's iconic brick wall—a feature that now seems required décor at comedy clubs everywhere—is a balding, gray-bearded man in the Semi-Official Uniform of Stand-up: Black tee shirt and jeans. His non-English accent, immediately recognizable as Middle Eastern, is surprisingly pronounced for a U.S. comic.

Erik Angel is Jewish, but most of his material is not the standard American Jewish stand-up diet of ambitious mothers, or anxiety over being in a minority with a tragic history. Instead, Angel's humor—sometimes dark, always enlightening—springs from his identity as an Israeli:

I was born and raised in a culture that believes you don't need to speak if you can say the exact same word shouting. This is why when people see two Israelis talking, they think we are having a fight. We're not having a fight. Of course, at some point we're going *to have a fight...*

Through midlife, Angel was doing pretty well in Israel as an actor and recording artist (he released three albums in Hebrew), but comedy proved to be his ultimate passion. He moved to the U.S. and set up shop in New York City—perhaps the world's toughest landing strip for fledgling comics.

"I have a real business sense for doing things you cannot make money at," he tells me with perfect deadpan timing.

My looping voyage through America's divisions and hopeful reunion has taken an early virtual turn: The nomadic life of a standup comic has required us to meet via Zoom. Angel is, for the moment, at his home in Manhattan's Upper West Side. Over Angel's shoulder, from behind his desk, peers a poster of Franz Kafka—who, history tells us, could not get through public readings of his dystopian novel *The Trial* without breaking down into uncontrollable laughter. ("I don't understand," I can imagine the existentialist author asking his bemused audience, "what part of 'He had ten different ways of killing himself' do you not find amusing?")

Luckily, U.S. audiences have found Angel's humor more accessible than Kafka's. By 2019, he was making audiences laugh at clubs throughout the U.S. and Canada:

So, I moved to America, and I discovered that I'm Jewish! Forty years I was an Israeli, now I'm the Jew. And I quickly learned everything is my fault. Suddenly I control the money here? Why nobody told me that? I control Hollywood? You mean they keep shooting Fast and Furious *movies because of me...?*

Along the way, Angel encountered comedians who, like him, were Middle Eastern transplants—only many of them were from countries that are, shall we say, not Jewish state-friendly. Often, they and Angel would appear on the same bill.

Great comedy is often all about tension. Why not, Angel reasoned, mine that tension in the most positive way possible? He began pitching an idea to Muslim and Jewish comedians: a traveling show in which they would share the stage and, without stepping on each other's cultural toes, explore the universality of Funny.

"We had one rule," he says. "No Politics, Just Laughs."

And so, Comedy for Peace was born. Since 2019, Angel has ushered a rotating crew of Muslim, Hindu, Jewish, and Christian comics from coast to coast, proving that humor is truly the universal language (in this case, so long as you speak English). As Angel had hoped, the group's comedic observations proved to be defiantly ethnic, yet refreshingly universal:

Zahra Ali, Muslim American comic:

I love that movie A Christmas Story*! Every year I'd post on my social media. "I want a Red Ryder BB gun too!" But this year I can't do that, or else I'll end up on some Muslim data base. 'Cause I am the scary shade of brown. It's called "ISIS Brown."*

"We are," Angel tells me, "each one of us, telling our stories, focusing on our backgrounds and where we come from. There's no dirty humor in our shows; we're not trying to make anybody uncomfortable. Not in that way, anyway. It's the opposite, really: The more we laugh about ourselves, and about each other, the more we learn about each other."

In some ways, Comedy for Peace is what United Nations General Assembly meetings would be like if the speeches were accompanied by rim shots.

"I say, 'Don't come to our shows for a fight,'" Angel says. "'If you want to fight, do it before or do it after. But come sit with us for two hours, under one roof, and we'll show you how easy it is to just have fun and forget about the news, or what people have told you at home.' If we all just stay in our tribes, the world is going to get worse."

Usama Siddiquee, Muslim Bengali-American comic:

Every week my dad would tell us, "When I came to this country I had only five dollars in my pocket." I say, "Dad, how did you leave the airport? Terminal D to Terminal E is a ten dollar cab ride"...

Kalid Rahmaanere, Muslim-African American comic:

My parents converted to Islam back in the '60s. Because just being Black wasn't difficult enough.

Steve Marshall, Jewish-American comic:

My parents taught me the value of money the old-fashioned Jewish way. They withheld taxes from my allowance.

It turns out that among comedians, clueless parents are the secret sauce of commonality.

Paul Schissler

"Yeah, parents are great," says Paul Schissler, one of Comedy for Peace's resident Christian comics. "I think we've all got something about our parents, and audiences seem to latch onto the fact that it's a common theme for us."

Schissler and I are some 3,000 miles from New York, sitting on the sunny patio of Highly Likely, a coffee shop in Los Angeles' Highland Park neighborhood. (Yes, I know this abrupt change in locale is wreaking havoc on my "journey-'round-the-country" conceit. Can we all just agree that we live in a period when time and space are fungible, at best? And the fact is, comedy troupes don't stick together like Post-Its. We'll get back to our travelogue format presently, trust me.)

I'll be the first to admit to an unfounded stereotype, but I've known a fair share of comedians, and it's always seemed to me that West Coast comics are decidedly more laid-back than their East Coast brethren.

Schissler gives me no reason to disavow my reasoned assignment of personality traits: Lanky and leisurely in a collared polo shirt, he could just as easily be my five-year-old grandson's affable T-ball coach. Still, like so many comedians—no matter what their ethnicity—Schissler's humor is largely rooted in childhood wounds.

Raised by a single mom after his father left the family, Schissler assumed the role of family pressure relief valve.

"My role," he recalls, "was to make Mom laugh."

My mom had to teach me how to shave. But she did a really good job. 'Cause now I have really smooth legs...

As one of Comedy for Peace's newer members, Schissler says he realized almost immediately that moms are, hands-down, the common denominator in cross-cultural humor.

"The Jewish mom, the Muslim mom, the Southern U.S. Christian mom? It's all the same thing," he says. "When are you going to get married?' 'Hey, grandchildren!' Our moms are all the same; they provide us all with the same points of injury, the same love points."

Raised in Florida, Schissler won a standup comedy competition during his senior year at Auburn University. He did not even need to tell me this was one of the worst things that ever happened to him: The last thing any young man needs, after all, is to be told he's the best at anything. From that point, only seas of molten lava lie ahead.

"I bought a one-way ticket to New York…and failed for so, so long," he says, his gaze lingering on his coffee. At a nearby table, a young woman may be breaking up with her boyfriend. I see Shissler's eyes shift, as if he's making mental notes for a future routine.

"I did my first open mic night there and I left thinking, 'I don't even know what comedy is,'" he finally says.' I didn't even know who I wanted to be."

I tell Schissler about a time in the late 1970s when I went to see Rodney Dangerfield perform at the Sunrise Musical Theater in Florida. The opening act was this lanky guy in a white suit. He was funny, I thought, but was also desperately trying to be Steve Martin.

The guy was Jim Carrey.

Schissler's eyes light up.

"I was like that," he says. "I kept trying to settle on a style. I was still me, but different versions of me. I tried to do Jim Carrey. I tried to be Stephen Wright for a little while…"

Like all successful artists, Schissler finally settled into a personality close to his real one: A dad and husband whose Christianity does not inoculate him from the funny frustrations of life.

As a millennial, I identify with Jesus. Because I, too, have never owned a home…

Schissler is what the trade calls a "clean" comic, one who knows how to work a pale kind of blue for early evening adult audiences and church groups.

Paul Shissler on stage

I lost my virginity to my wife when I was twenty-seven. And believe it or not, just because you dream about something for two decades does not mean you're going to be good at it...

That made him a perfect fit with Comedy for Peace. While the group has been an in-demand ticket at multiple New York Comedy Festivals, during the rest of the year, at least so far, most performances have been for Jewish groups. "Still, there always seems to be at least one Christian in the audience," says Schissel. "When I start, I'll say, 'Yeah, I'm the New Testament portion of the show. Are there any Christians here? Any? Anyone?' No one puts their hand up. But then, after the show, there's always one person who comes up to me and kind of whispers, '*I was the one.*'"

Usama Siddiquee, Muslim American comic:

After 9/11 my mother was a little scared. She said, Usama, do you want to change your name to something a little less Muslim? I swear to God, she said, "How about Hussein?"

Atheer Yacoub, Palestinian American comic:

I said, "Dad, you're the only Arab Muslim in an all-white neighborhood. You don't need a gun for protection. You're the reason everyone else has one."

Comedy can arise from our discomfort zones, and beyond the laughs. Comedy for Peace does not pretend the sometimes-lethal pressures of the outside world aren't authentic.

That reality becomes most evident during the Q and A sessions that follow each show—especially since October 7, 2023, when terrorists attacked and slaughtered hundreds of Israelis at a music festival, and Israel responded with a massive, unrelenting attack on the Palestinian Gaza Strip.

"The show is still fun — and funny," says Angel on our Zoom call from New York.

"But the Q and A—that has become more emotional. The Israel-Hamas conflict deeply affects people on both sides. The thing is, they arrive without any real knowledge of each other. On some level, they may be afraid of people who are not like them. And now, those things are cranked way up."

Both the questions and the answers, he says, come from the same place: An exasperation with the persistence of evil in a world of people who, for the most part, just want to get along.

"It's coming from the sad reality that we see all the time—that out in the world and even here in America, there are people who just want to control other people," Angel says.

Power really is the ultimate aphrodisiac, Comedy for Peace seems to be saying, if by aphrodisiac you mean the ability to pummel people into submission.

"These people may try to gain power over others through being a governor, or a premier, or a president," he says "But in the end, the only thing those power-hungry people want is to tell you what you can do—and we happen to live at a time when that desire is becoming extreme."

As difficult as the Q and A's may be, however, the release comes after the show, as the cast and audience simply mingle and chat.

"I see it all the time," Angel says. "People from different groups, standing together and talking, as if the divisions the world is trying to force on them don't exist."

Angel closes his eyes and recalls a poignant post-performance moment he experienced in Florida, following a set that included the Pakistani American comic Gibran Saleem:

Gibran Saleen:

My parents had an arranged marriage in Pakistan. When they got to the States my dad said, "What do you want to see first?" And my mom said, "Other people."

"An old man approached me," says Angel. "He said, 'I have to admit,

I'm eighty-two years old, and I've never met a Muslim guy in my life. And now I'm in love with Gibram Saleem. He's such a wonderful human being.'

"And then he said something I found really poignant: 'I wish things were different.'

"Well, so do I. And maybe we can help make them at least a little different."

Angel is the first to admit that Comedy for Peace can't make everything better in a world that seems determined to drive wedges between people. But he's certain that, show by show, the art of comedy will inevitably open the hearts of people who, under most circumstances, would have nothing to do with each other.

"The differences among us come from fear," he says. "They come from ignorance. They even sometimes come from laziness: I'm here in my group. In my tribe. Don't ask me to walk outside that.

"For me, nothing could be more boring. I want to know what that other guy thinks is funny. I want to taste his food; to see what kind of ice cream he likes. I want to laugh with him and enjoy the fact that we are two human beings, breathing the same air.

"We need to see the *real* reality—not what the politicians and big business are telling us is reality."

Angel performed some shows in Paris during the 2024 Olympics, and he recalls visiting a Lebanese restaurant near his hotel.

"I was warned before I got to Paris that I should not tell anyone where I was from," he says. "That's kind of easy for me, because for some reason people look at me and assume I'm from Germany or Sweden. Don't ask me why, I don't know."

As Angel stood at a counter of an Arab restaurant, waiting for his takeout order, the owner approached him and asked where he was from. Angel responded he was from America, and nothing more.

The restaurant owner gave Angel a sidelong glance.

"Okay, okay," he persisted. "But where are you *from*?'"

Angel hesitated, but he felt compelled to respond.

"Listen, I'm really hungry," he said. "I just don't want to get thrown out of here."

The owner stared him down.

"Listen," he said, "this is a house of peace."

Finally, Angel admitted to being Israeli. The guy smiled broadly.

"You are the first person to come in here who's had the courage to say that in a long time," he said, and led Angel to a table.

"He took out some dates, gave me a drink, and spoiled me with dessert," Angel recalls softly. "We had such a beautiful conversation. We took pictures (which he asked me not to post online). And he couldn't believe I even knew some Arabic.

"I left with a big bag of food, and with tears in my eyes."

That's the driving force behind Comedy for Peace, he says: People just want to connect, and they're desperately seeking channels through which they can do that without judgment.

"I hate Hamas," he says. "I saw what they did to my people. I want to kill them all myself. But not all Palestinians are Hamas. All Muslims are not Hamas. They just want to raise their families; to enjoy life."

I can sense Angel, who knows he's here to talk about comedy, is suddenly a bit worried he's wandered down a non-parallel path. He tries to lighten the mood.

"It's like me and my wife," he chuckles. "I love my wife. I care for her. But sometimes, you know, I cannot stand her."

***

The power of comedy, Angel concludes, goes far beyond the laughter. He recalls a Comedy for Peace show in Fort Lauderdale, Florida. The performance was sponsored by a local Jewish Community Center, but they held it in a true comedy club with 400 seats.

"The show went really good, of course," he says, "but the best thing happened two days later: The JCC and the Muslims had a meeting in a local mosque, and they decided to establish a soccer team for Muslim and Jewish kids."

He laughs. And it's not a ha-ha kind of laugh. It's a laugh of wonderment.

"It's just like this big, big flower that's growing from the ground."

Funny thing, comedy.

The Hunt Club

Delaware: The First Rule About Hunt Club

(You don't talk about Hunt Club)

The deer burger is surprisingly tasty. *Meaty* is the way I'd describe it. A lot meatier than the ground beef that comes wrapped in cellophane at the grocery store.

"Glad you like it!" says Elwood, a retired southern Delaware postmaster. He's just grilled up a batch of deer burgers out back and brought them into the clubhouse on a paper plate. The ones on top are still sizzling.

"You want a Captain and Coke?" Before I can answer, he heads for the well-stocked bar to mix me a drink.

Halfway across the large, low-ceilinged meeting room, Joe, who owns a taxidermy business, is nursing a drink of his own.

"That meat you buy in the store, it's got no taste at all," he says. "I just bought a whole cow from a guy in Virginia. After you eat that, you'll never eat store meat again! I got steaks this size!" He holds his hands a ridiculously wide distance apart.

"You're eating like Fred Flintstone!" laughs Paul, a retired New York state cop.

"Yeah!" Joe guffaws. "Just like Fred and Barney!"

Delaware, my home state, less than a day's drive from Asheville, has always sat astride the North and the South: During the Civil War, families were torn asunder by sons choosing up sides between the Union and the Confederacy. To this day, there are friction points, and among them is the whole idea of killing animals in the wild for food.

This hunt club building used to be a gas station and garage. Until a few years ago, the old pumps were still standing out front. It's a nondescript, windowless cinder-block affair with narrow doors. For passersby, the only signs of life are a few cars parked out front and, from behind the building, the scent of deer burger wafting from Elwood's grill.

The Hunt Club is not located in an actual hunting ground. This particular club, with about fifty members who pay $800 in annual dues, leases tracts of land from farmers and forestry businesses throughout coastal Delaware — about 1,000 acres in all.

"That sounds like a lot," says Paul. "But we lose at least one tract every year."

The club keeps track of who is hunting where, to prevent hunters from clumping together.

Inside, the heads of a dozen or so prize deer, most with impressive racks of antlers, stretch proudly along one wall; on an opposite wall hang trophies from some members' African hunts: impala, kudu, springbok, blue wildebeest.

"These must be real prize trophies," I observe, pretending to know what I'm talking about.

Paul chuckles.

"Well, at best these are the second-best," he says. "The real prizes are hanging in their homes, trust me!"

I can barely imagine myself in a more foreign environment. Growing up a few miles from the George Washington Bridge in New Jersey, my idea of big game was Monopoly. The only gun I ever fired had a cork in the end of it. And the only animal head I've ever hung on a wall was that of a small alligator I bought at a Stuckey's in Yeehaw Junction, Florida.

Yet here are these guys, welcoming me into their inner sanctum, friendly as can be, even though they know I'm a writer — and not the kind who works for *Field & Stream*. I'm a city boy. A glance at my social media feed would ignite 1000-watt red lights in any Conservative control room.

But I feel welcome here. These guys want to tell their story. They want to be understood by people like me. And the mere fact that my presence here is such an anomaly is an indictment of those who think they are too morally superior to listen.

I hear gunshots!

On any given day, words to that effect pop up on social media where I live in coastal Delaware. Often, the alerts are accompanied by comments such as "I left the city to get away from gunshots and now gang warfare is erupting right here at the beach." Newcomers, it seems, usually arrive in Delaware blissfully unaware that the hunters were here first, and I mean *really* first: Even before guns arrived on ships from Europe, hunters were trekking among the creeks and woodlands shooting arrows and, earlier than that, thrusting spears.

In recent centuries, the biggest local game has been the ancestors of those deer heads now peering at me from the clubhouse walls. Just a few decades ago, great swaths of woodland pressed close to the Delaware shore and bays, making the area a prime hunting ground not just for locals, but also for sportsmen and women from all over the Northeast, who were seeing their local wildlands pushed out by development.

And there was a bonus: While urbanites and their suburban brethren increasingly looked down on hunting as a savage caveman-like throwback (I blame *Bambi*), native Delawareans — as members of a historically agrarian culture — understood the essential roles hunting played not only in providing sustenance, but also in preserving the health of animals in the wild: Too many large animals in one place inevitably leads to scarce food supplies, starvation and disease.

Do I need to mention that things have changed?

Not among the men who are eating, drinking and sharing stories around this table in the Hunt Club. But outside these doors, while the wilderness is fast disappearing, a groundswell of high-minded opposition to hunting — ignorant of its mission, radical and often abusive in its assignment of shame — is spreading like a forest wildfire.

Supposed animal lovers harass hunters in the field, banging pans and honking horns.

"We've got no sign on this building," says Paul. "Otherwise, within a week there'd be red paint splashed on the walls."

More often than not, those protesters are worked into a lather by anti-hunting screeds written by guys who look and sound a lot like me.

That is why I've agreed not to share the club's name and location. And it's why on this Thursday evening, when a dozen or so members would ordinarily show up for the group's weekly food-and-booze get-together, only four have come.

There's a *writer* here.

***

Luckily, I have a patron.

It's important to understand just how difficult it is for a non-hunter to break into the reclusive hunt club culture. I'd been trying for months. For one thing, hunt clubs don't generally list themselves online. They don't have public phone numbers. Notes left in rusty mailboxes along the dirt roads leading into hunt club properties go unanswered. An inquiry I posted on Facebook yielded just a couple of semi-leads — people offering to approach local hunters on my behalf — and all of them came up dry.

Then I remembered Joe. A few years ago, I wrote a short magazine article about Joe, who had recently opened a taxidermy studio next to his home near Harbeson. Re-reading the article, and satisfied that I had neither utterly embarrassed myself nor painted hunters as bloodthirsty killers, I gave him a call: Could he somehow get me into a hunt club?

"Sure!" he shot back with his rural Long Island accent. "Come on over Thursday!"

And so here I am, a stranger in a strange land, probably overthinking what I can and cannot ask about.

One thing that's definitely off-limits: the occupations of the club members who are still working. Despite the fact that hunting is, perhaps, the oldest human occupation; even though hunting is arguably protected in the U.S. Constitution's Second Amendment; and although the state of Delaware has entire departments dedicated to little more than guaranteeing the health, safety and enjoyment of hunters, the social stigma that has arrived along with those moving vans from New York, Philadelphia and Washington, D.C., has all but pushed the hunters—who, I will mention again, were here first—underground. Stories abound of people in the real estate business—some of whose families have lived in and hunted this area for well over a century—who feel they must hide the fact that they're hunters for fear they'll either lose clients or never see potential ones.

So, if you want to join a hunt club, you have to, perhaps appropriately, go hunting for one. And even when you find a friend of a friend who has a brother who's in a Delaware hunt club, membership isn't automatic. The number of acres a club hunts largely dictates how many members it can support.

"It took me years to get into this club," says Joe. "And I'm a friggin' *taxidermist*!"

"Look, I'm an ex-cop," Paul chimes in, "so I don't care what people think. But it's two different worlds. There are a lot of people who are in businesses who would lose a lot of their livelihood if they told people they were hunters. And it's all because thirty percent of the population is ignorant, and they'll be mad at you."

Until this moment, Paul has been leaning back in his chair, chatting amiably. But now he's leaning forward. His hand wraps tightly around a can of Miller Lite.

"Those people have to actually go underground because of the bullies," he says. "They just bully you into doing whatever their way of thinking is. 'We know we can't change the laws, but we can shame you and bully you and dox you. We'll take business away from you.'"

"That's what they do, and it only takes one or two of 'em to push you underground, if you're trying to make a living."

The problem is by no means isolated among conservative hunters. There are, to be sure, uncounted liberal hunters across the country, but even they have been chased into the woods, hounded by fellow progressives.

A Google search yields the website of The Liberal Gun Club—"to provide a pro-Second Amendment voice for left-of-center gun owners"—but click on the site and you will come upon one dead link after another.

Public attempts by liberals to portray themselves as hunters usually come up something short of authentic, and often downright comical. Democratic Presidential candidate John Kerry didn't help his doomed candidacy—and may have hurt it—when he turned up at an Ohio grocery store and drawled, in his best Yale manner, "Can I get me a hunting license here?" Later, he refused to be photographed with the bird he'd shot. More recently, in 2018 Pennsylvania Democratic congressman Matt Cartwright admitted he was taking up deer hunting purely to appeal to conservative voters (it may have worked—he was re-elected).

True liberal hunters have, perhaps, an even more difficult time finding a safe place to share their passion. Consider the "About This Group" Facebook statement for a page called "Liberal Hunters of North America," which has about 1,000 members:

"This group was created in 2019 when my life was threatened for my liberal views in another Facebook hunting group…I notified the Administrator who told me the comment would stay, and that maybe I just didn't fit his group."

The saddest thing about all this is the most obvious point: Both conservative and liberal hunters are absolutely, one hundred percent aligned in their passion. The opportunities for finding common cause, for discovering unexpected friendships, are tangible. But suspicions born of political conflict have pushed them into sociologically isolated duck blinds.

Part of the problem, according to writer Oliver Stanley, is that over the past century cities have become bastions of liberalism while the wide-open spaces—where hunting happens—are largely conservative.

"Of course it's possible to be a liberal hunter," Stanley wrote on the website Quartz. "Hunting doesn't belong to conservatives any more than hiking belongs to liberals.

"But perhaps the solution, or the beginning of the solution, to America's gun problem will come not from further entrenchment into our positions, but more crossing over to the other side. Maybe the solution isn't just more conservatives willing to consider gun control, but also more liberals learning how to hunt."

***

The main thing hunters want non-hunters to understand—and something hunters, by now, almost despair of ever getting them to understand—is how much they love nature. And I mean *love* it. The huggiest tree-hugger at Berkeley would have their mind blown if they truly understood the passion these guys have for the outdoors.

Annual hunting limits are set not by hunters, but by wildlife biologists, who calculate how many animals must be harvested in order to maintain a healthy population—and it's hunters who are out there in the field, making sure those limits are not surpassed. In Delaware, a hunters' group called Whitetails Unlimited raises more than $100,000 a year for wildlife conservation projects.

And then there's the constellation of fees hunters pay, nearly all of which are poured back into state wildlife management services.

"The uneducated person thinks we go out there and just shoot everything up," says Paul. "Well, we have about fifty-five members here, and I believe we shot twelve bucks last year."

So, the first rule about Hunt Club may have less to do with hunting and everything to do with the crunch of leaves beneath your feet, and the canopy of trees above your head, and the whisper of wind flitting across an open field.

On some of his best hunting days, Paul says, he hasn't shot a thing.

"If you've had a tough day, if you need to take a deep breath and reset your life, go sit in the woods," he says. The other guys turn to him, as if there is a benediction being offered. Even those deer on the walls seem to be paying attention.

"I don't care if it's just for an hour or two. So many people tell me about their morning walks on the beach and their outside exercise routines, but I can tell you no one has seen as many red sunsets and icy sunrises as I have.

"Yeah. When you're in the woods like that, sitting still and silent, you see things you're not supposed to see. The animals do what they always do when you're not there. You can wait and count 'em — twenty-five, thirty different kinds of animals.

"The sun comes up, and I think about my life and I give thanks. Then I stand up and go home, and I see my family, and I start my day.

"That's being a hunter. What's better than that?"

No hunter, left or right, would argue with that.

Betsey Coffia & John Roth

Michigan: Swing State

When the Margins are Slim, Compromise is the Rule

Washington, Delaware and New York have their share of water, of course, but the first thing I notice as I roll into Traverse City, Michigan: There's water *everywhere*. The long, slender finger of Grand Traverse Bay points at me as I drive west along its southern tip toward town, the bay's shoreline dotted with tall trees and punctuated by private docks, boats bobbing all the way to the horizon.

Presently, the bay shore is behind me, and I ascend into Traverse City proper, a pleasing blend of homes, shops, and county government buildings. But soon I glance out my right window and find I'm once again at the fingernail end of a long, slender body of water that stretches to infinity, almost identical to the one I've just left behind.

For newcomers, this disorienting déjà vu takes some getting used to: It's the result of the Traverse City shoreline being interrupted by a twenty-mile-long, one-mile-wide splinter of land that splits Grand Traverse Bay into two skinny slivers, each with a unique microclimate that, depending on the time of year, renders one slightly warmer or infinitesimally cooler than the other.

This barely measurable shifting of climate isn't a bad allegory for the political atmosphere of Michigan, certainly one of the most unpredictable swing states in the country.

"Swing State" is probably too dramatic a term to describe Michigan. The phrase implies a political environment where a great pendulum sweeps to and fro, carrying the electorate on a wild carnival ride of ideological extremus.

But it doesn't take much to turn the political tide in Michigan, among the nation's most closely divided states. In 2024, Republicans accounted for 49.64 percent of the statewide vote; Democrats 48.23 percent. Accordingly, Michigan is not a swing state so much as a "nudge state." No one political party can let itself get too comfortable in the catbird seat.

Traverse City is, for my money, Michigan's most livable burg: a sliver of downtown nestled in the arms of Lake Michigan's Grand Traverse Bay, surrounded by thousands of acres of its famous cherry trees—and more recently, vineyards. (Increasingly, those cherry orchards are being uprooted in favor of grape vines, which thrive in the region's lake-moderated seasons.)

As in much of the nation, Michigan's cities trend liberal and the rural areas skew conservative. But a small city like Traverse, surrounded by farms, has a day-to-day mix of both groups doing business and generally mingling with each other. That makes the local political climate particularly prickly—and that's why you'll find, in adjacent districts, state representatives who face the choice of working together or staring each other down in a perpetual standoff of legislative stasis.

At the moment I'm visiting Michigan, for example, the previous Democratic legislative majority is in the process of reluctantly handing control to the Republicans, who eked out a victory the previous Fall.

But I hear no gloating from Republican Rep. John Roth, who represents Traverse City…and no bitterness from Democratic Rep. Betsy Coffia, who represents the district next door. Chatting with both of them, I get the distinct impression each is keenly aware of their party's tentative hold on power—and the accompanying mandate to find common ground in trying to serve their constituents.

In 2024, as contentious a political year as the U.S. has ever seen, the pair cosponsored a plan to help local resorts sidestep a nineteenth century state law that was preventing them from operating under twenty-first century business realities. The proposal passed the state house unanimously.

Despite the storm clouds of partisanship gathering across the continent, Roth says, “There is no question in my mind that the people want the parties to work together. Everyone is worried about what’s happening in Washington, DC, but I say, ‘Stop. There are a lot of people in politics who are looking for a balance.’

“In fact, here in Michigan, I’m looking forward to two really good years, because with our slim majority we’re all going to have to work together.”

Even when Democrats held the majority in the Michigan state house from 2020 to 2024, Coffia was in a minority of sorts. Unusually, in Michigan, state representatives caucus not only by party, but also by region. So, although she was elected into a Democratic House majority in 2022, Coffia found herself the lone Democrat in Michigan’s Northern Caucus.

“I was the only Democrat for one-hundred miles in any direction,” she says. “So, I had a choice to make: I could go it alone or I could work with my Republican colleagues on things on which we have commonality. And there are a lot of them: We have infrastructure issues. We have a childcare crisis. We have a mental health crisis and a housing crisis.”

Issues like that, she says, have nothing to do with partisanship.

“The people are just saying, ‘You work on that!’”

In Michigan, at least, Roth says he sees the tide of partisanship turning for the better. Just two years ago, activists from both sides of the aisle—roughly ten or twenty out of 110 legislature members—thought they saw a window to push through legislation that pandered to the extremes.

“Finally, the rest of us just said, ‘Hey, let’s work together and get things done,’” she recalls. “And in this last election, there were fewer activists elected, and I’ve seen more people willing to be bipartisan. I have hope for that.”

To be sure, the two major parties in Michigan retain their core values regarding the size and influence of government and appropriate levels of taxation.

“I’m not a hugely political person,” says Roth, “but I do know how to speak the language, and I’ll speak it when I need to. But these days we just have a very good feel in the House.”

Coffia points to her working relationship with John Damoose, a conservative Republican member of Michigan’s state senate who has publicly stated he and Coffia will never agree on guns and abortion.

“And he’s right, we won’t,” says Coffia. “But together we got $15 million for a Great Lakes fresh water research center and $5 million for teacher housing."

The best news, she says, is that if you look behind the performative partisan politicking, you can often find similar cooperation blossoming even on the national level: Michigan Democratic Senator Debbie Stabenow worked with uber-conservative Missouri Senator Roy Blunt to support 24/7 mental health care. Far-left independent Vermont Senator Bernie Sanders and Senator Josh Hawley, a stalwart Trump Republican, co-sponsored a bill to cap credit card interest rates. Even liberal firebrand Rep. Alexandria Ocasio-Cortez of New York teamed up with conservative provocateur Matt Gates—then still a Republican congressman from Florida—to co-sponsor a bill preventing members of Congress from trading stocks. The bill was wildly popular among both Republicans and Democrats.

"It's not always easy to work together," adds Roth, "but it's worth the effort. In a closely divided government, maybe not as much policy gets passed as when there's a lopsided majority. But trust me, it will be better policy. No question in my mind."

***

Of course, it's not difficult to cite states (*cough-New York and California-cough*) where opposite-number representatives in adjacent districts regularly tear each other new ones. But it's my observation that those pugilistic politicos most often pop up in states where one party keeps the other in a stranglehold. To successfully represent the good people of Michigan it seems, you have to echo their general willingness to get along with each other.

I'd like you to meet George Champlin and Kirk Mallow. George grew up in the arch-conservative town of Jackson, Michigan and moved to Traverse City in 1987. He remains decidedly right-wing to this day, now retired after twenty-five years working for the county. Kirk has worked as a custodian and maintenance man in the Traverse City area for more than thirty years. He's also gay, liberal, and in the past few years has become increasingly anxious about the future of the country's LGBTQ community.

Yet here they are, sitting across from me in a long, windowed wine tasting room at Traverse City's Mari Vineyards, a re-created Umbrian castle on a hill overlooking Lake Michigan's Grand Traverse Bay.

Kirk Mallow & George Champlin (photo by Mike Kent)

It is winter, so outside those windows Mari's vines are covered with snow—which turns out not to be a bad thing when you're growing cold weather-tolerant grapes. I am sipping a fine glass of Estate 2021 Bel Tramonto; they are nursing tall glasses of water, maybe because it's barely noon. Don't judge me.

Sitting on the table between us is the largest Bavarian pretzel my eyes have ever seen; its open spaces stuffed with generous helpings of charcuterie items. We are all picking at it, like vultures on a deer carcass.

George is in his seventies, a long gray beard covering his chin, a Toys for Tots baseball cap covering his head. Kirk, fifty-ish, sports a full beard and a dark t-shirt. George leans back and drapes his left arm over the chair next to him; Kirk leans forward, his elbows on the table, fingers laced together.

This is no gimmicky oil-and-water get-together. George and Kirk have been buddies for years. The two were brought together by their shared passion for the Holiday charity Toys for Tots, and that casual connection blossomed into a lifelong friendship.

"Kirk and I are probably as far apart in politics and stuff like that as you can get," says George. "But we're friends. Some other places you might find people trying to trigger each other, but we don't do that. We focus on the things that bring us together."

Kirk nods.

The trouble, George tells me with a furrowed brow, is that people are tragically more willing to believe what they hear about people—rather than what they see with their own eyes.

"I look at Kirk," he says, "and I simply see a man who has a heart for helping kids."

Both men acknowledge there are hopelessly polarized elements in Michigan that could never understand their friendship. But that's the distinct minority, they insist. Michigan politics has a long history of bipartisanship—beginning with 1970's Detroit Mayor Coleman Young, a disruptive liberal Democrat, and Republican Governor Bill Milliken, who struck up an unlikely alliance to save Detroit from bankruptcy.

"It's just the way people are brought up here," says George. "We watch out for each other, no matter what." People who need help, he says, are simply people who need help. "We're not gonna worry about whether they're Republican or Democrat, or if they're straight or gay or bisexual. I've seen it time and time again around here; people step up."

A gust of Lake Michigan wind slaps against the window behind Kirk and George. They turn together to look toward the water. I sneak a bite of pretzel.

Why, I ask, has that attitude not sustained itself as the default position in American society? Their answer is unanimous, and expressed in unison: "Social media."

Both bemoan the hyper-aggressive nature of social media, where people hide behind their keyboards or phones while hurling bombs at each other. It's worthwhile, Kirk says, to take a breath before you post a critical comment.

"I know sometimes I see something political on Facebook that I immediately want to share," he says. "But I'll wait a minute, and very often I'll just decide not to do it. I have friends who would be hurt by that comment, and why would I want to hurt my friends? In fact, why would I want to hurt anybody?"

I leave George and Kirk to pick through the remains of our prodigious pretzel and trudge back to my car, unwilling to believe what the local vintners claim: that the wet rag of a wind whipping up from protected Traverse Bay is, in any way, warmer than the ones produced by the frigid Great Lake beyond.

But the glow of conviviality, Traverse City style, persists. As I navigate the winding roads back to town, I can't help but take note that—popular vote-wise, at least—the nation as a whole tends to echo the razor-thin division in Michigan's electorate. Why can't our national politics enjoy the same we're-all-in-this-together optimism?

Are we incapable of it on a macro level? Or are we just believing what we hear, and not what we see?

Kateri Klingele Pinell

Wisconsin: Women and Children First

Agreement Beyond Abortion

Do you have trouble confusing Michigan and Wisconsin? I am so, so ashamed to admit this, but even as my editor read this manuscript, he kept leaving me notes: "Don't you mean Michigan?" "Aren't you supposed to be in Wisconsin?"

I could explain that both states are shaped like mittens, and that's the source of my issue, but the reality is I suffer from a most common form of Coastal Dementia. For me, and for a long time, Michigan and Wisconsin—let alone Nebraska and Iowa—existed as fantasy lands akin to Narnia and Terabithia; vaguely familiar, somewhat undefined realms populated by a few notable characters behind whom milled vast, faceless, supporting casts of subjects and enablers.

Well, I recently discovered that not only is Wisconsin *right next door* to Michigan, but like their mitten-y neighbors, Wisconsinites have a true heart for finding common ground, even in the face of intractable differences.

Take what may well be the defining divisive issue of our time: Abortion.

Unavoidably, I've been told all my adult life, when you try to strike a balance on abortion you are foiled by the intransigent barrier of two discreet

Ali Muldrow

groups that not only hold fiercely felt personal convictions—but who also harbor similarly strident opinions about those who disagree with them.

Abortion rights supporters, the culture at large tells us, insist they are protecting the health and rights of women...and that those who feel otherwise are primarily intent on subjugating women, rendering them little more than human incubators, *à la Handmaid's Tale*.

Abortion opponents, on the other hand, are said to be adamant that their only concern is saving the lives of unborn children, who they hold are every bit as human at the moment of conception as they will be the day they get their driver's licenses. Those who disagree, they generally believe, are selfishly sacrificing the lives of children for personal convenience.

I must hasten to add we often hear of wide agreement between the two groups regarding abortion to save the life of a mother: President Ronald Reagan himself, whose "Abortion and the Conscience of a Nation" remains required reading among pro-life activists, cited the Biblical right to self-defense as a rationale for life-saving abortions. But many abortion abolitionists oppose even that level of latitude, and among those who accept it there remain disagreements when it comes to defining just *when* a mother's life is endangered by a pregnancy.

Overall, I was convinced, Pro-Life and Pro-Choice people have a difficult enough time living in the same country, much less sitting down in the same room.

I've never been so glad to be proven wrong by two extraordinary young women who, according to most current cultural norms, should absolutely, positively hate each other.

Ali Mudrow lives in Madison, Wisconsin's state capital. She became pregnant as a teenager and, navigating the medical bureaucracy on her own, obtained an abortion—a decision she found empowering. Today she's executive director of a women's health foundation and treasurer of the Madison Board of Education.

Kateri Klingele Pinell also grew up in Madison, one of eleven children. She became pregnant as a teen, kept the baby and married the father—and after having another child with him left the marriage under a cloud of domestic violence. A single mom through graduate school, she's now happily remarried and a clinical mental health professional who believes people should live free of violence from the start of their lives, which she views as the moment of conception. (In keeping with that philosophy, she also opposes capital punishment.) The dominant present-day narrative—indeed, the narrative that had me despairing over ever being able to write a chapter about abortion—would pit these two women at each other's throats. But on Mother's Day 2025, the pair launched a joint campaign across the state of Wisconsin, calling for enhanced government-sponsored postpartum care for new mothers.

They called the initiative "Medicaid for Mother's Day." The hashtag read: #betterthanabouquet.

"This Mother's Day," Ali wrote on the local news site Madison360, "Mothers from the left, the right, and everywhere in between are coming together to call for an extension of post-partum Medicaid coverage. This display of collaboration across political differences is a reminder that—even in these polarized times—we must refuse to be enemies."

At the top of the article is a photo of Ali and Kateri, standing together on the state house steps, holding a cardboard sign reading "Medicaid for Mother's Day."

Now the two are paired up in an intensive lobbying campaign, trying to get reluctant state representatives to expand Medicare benefits for new mothers.

On the day I catch up with Kateri and Ali via teleconferencing, Ali is at home in Madison and Kateri is visiting Washington, DC, with her family.

"Ali is fiery, just like me," laughs Kateri. "We certainly have different views of things. But she's a phenomenal woman who passionately cares about doing what she believes is good."

Ali is equally magnanimous toward her political opposite.

"We're both moms of multiple children, people who have lived in poverty and survived domestic violence," she tells me. "The things we have in common are just as profound as the things that make us different. If you let yourself see someone holistically, you realize your lives intersect in a thousand ways."

It helps enormously that Ali and Katerie are that type of person who doesn't mind plunging head-first into an encounter with an other-thinking individual—not with a chip on their shoulder, but in a spirit of possible collaboration.

"I harbor no ill will for those who hold a different position than myself," says Kateri. "I may believe they're wrong. I may believe their position on abortion causes harm and violence. But they're individuals who are loved, and who have inherent dignity and worth. And I hope I can work with people from all backgrounds."

Speaking with these two women, I am struck by their shared penumbra of serenity. How, I wonder, can people who hold such unshakably different positions on a life-and-death subject nevertheless collaborate on a project that flits dangerously close to the white-hot flame that separates them?

The answer seems to come down to the pair's inherent willingness—and perhaps irresistible impulse—to relate to others.

Ali notes, for example, that even when others have a less-than-charitable attitude toward her, that's no reason to write them off.

"My favorite thing to do when someone insults me online," she says, leaning forward, "is to ask them if they want to go get coffee together."

And so, if you happen to spot Ali huddled over java at Madison's Lakeside Street Coffee House, it's entirely likely she's deep in conversation with someone who she was, just hours before, at odds with on social media.

Take the Facebook guy who, one morning, called Ali "ignorant."

I, of course, would have responded with a paralyzing, Noel Coward-class riposte like, "Not as Ignorant as…your MAMA!" Ali, on the other hand, took the high road.

"If you want me to learn more about the things you think I should learn more about," she wrote, "then let's get together."

At eleven a.m. that same morning, she recalls, "We were at Lakeside for coffee. We sat there for two hours talking about our views. And now he's one of my dearest friends."

Significantly, neither participant in the impromptu coffee klatch won the other over to their perspective.

"It wasn't a kumbaya moment," she says. "But he did come to understand that my perspective was valid, that my experiences were valid, that he had misunderstood where I was coming from."

When Ali's new friend had called her "ignorant," she came to understand, he wasn't trying to be cruel.

"He was just upset that I wasn't understanding something that was important to him."

***

You can see why Kateri and Ali were perfect candidates for a 2024 project aimed at finding some common ground—no matter how sparsely vegetated—among people with varied positions on abortion.

The effort was launched by Builders, a national coalition cofounded by Daniel Lubetzky, founder of the Kind snack bar company, and Lonnie Ali, widow of Muhammad Ali. A catalyst for open discussions among people of disparate viewpoints, Builders declares its intention is not necessarily to solve the conflicts that launch debate, but instead to chip away at the anger-inducing polarization that dogs those differences.

In early 2024, Builders enlisted people from across Wisconsin to participate in a workshop aimed at finding common ground regarding abortion. The resulting group—nine people supporting abortion rights; five firmly anti-abortion—spent their first day or so together explaining their positions and how they came to hold them. The next three days were roll-up-the-sleeves affairs, with the participants hashing out areas of agreement and finally fashioning possible legislation that would reflect their common ground.

Spoiler Alert: The group found no agreement whatsoever when it came to the base issue of abortion. But they did find common cause in ways to help prevent unwanted pregnancies and support mothers and children.

Perhaps most importantly, the two groups of people who many might offhandedly describe as "enemies" not only found areas of agreement—but also ended up, like Ali and Kateri, regarding each other as friends.

***

In the course of our teleconference, Ali, Kateri and I are joined by Jake VandenPlas, who lives up in the farmland of Door County, the thumb of Wisconsin's "mitten" projecting into the waters of Lake Michigan. A political conservative with a full, graying beard, he runs Door County Farm for Vets, which provides education and services for military veterans entering the field of agriculture.

Jake VandenPlas

Formerly, VandenPlas held moderately conservative views regarding abortion. Those positions have been somewhat softened, he confesses, through the influence of his wife, who obtained an abortion while in a previous, abusive relationship. Now when it comes to the issue, his focus is on finding ways to reduce the need for abortion by battling economic hardships, seeking harsher penalties for abusive partners, and providing greater access to birth control.

"Women need to have more choices regarding what's best for them," he says.

Long ago, I learned the hard way that a guy in the presence of many women discussing a hot-button issue that primarily involves women best serves the discussion by fading into the wallpaper. But this was not an option for Jake, and as I see him in a corner of my computer screen—his faithful farm dog lolling on a couch behind him—I express my condolences.

"Yeah," he says, scratching at his brow, "there's a lot of times when it's not really the proper position of a man to even have an opinion on things."

He brightens up a bit.

"But I did have some points to make about family planning, and the role that fathers play in the raising of kids and the support that we should be providing."

He harkens back to his first marriage, when his wife wanted to obtain an abortion and he opposed the idea.

"I knew I didn't have a choice in this whatsoever," he recalls softly. "But, you know, that was still my child. So, there are complexities to that argument. As a father, you want to at least have a seat at the table in the discussion."

Ali and Kateri, I can't help but notice, smile encouragingly, but do not weigh in on this particular observation.

How long, I wonder, did it take for the members of the group to get beyond their irreconcilable differences regarding abortion?

"I love that question," says Ali. "If you're asking how long it would take for me and Jake to dissect everything that makes us different, I'd say you're talking about a lifetime. Maybe two lifetimes! I mean, our differences aren't even restricted to reproductive health."

But the two share one essential value, she adds: A desire, through honest conversations, to devise solutions to common concerns. From Jake's perspective, that sometimes meant pushing the conversation ahead with concrete suggestions that were clearly non-starters for many in the group.

"I remember," Ali laughs, "when Jake announced, 'Why don't we just ban abortion after fifteen weeks?' And the people like me went, 'Absolutely not!' And Jake said, 'Okay, let's move on.'"

"All I wanted to do," Jake recalls, "was to just throw something on the table so we could keep the conversation moving forward."

"Right!" says Ali. "Jake was encouraging us to use that muscle; that muscle you use when you challenge an idea and keep trying something else."

At the heart of Jake's participation, she says, was his absolute refusal to give up. "He just kept chipping away at the conversation while listening to everyone in the room. We had so many of those challenging moments when people would push back. But not in a defensive way. They wouldn't get upset. They would just move on to, 'So what's an idea that would work for everybody?'"

Kateri, the firm abortion opponent, smiles when I ask her if she was afraid she'd be pressured to compromise her deeply held convictions.

"Well, I knew I would be," she says. "And I was. And that was difficult for me, because I frankly do care about what people think of me."

I glimpse Kateri's two young children chasing each other behind her chair. As she is momentarily distracted, I can't help but consider the pressures—economic and social—she endured raising them as a single mother, scraping together the means to support them while attending college and graduate school and launching a career.

"I said 'yes' to this project because I believe there is truth," she says. "And as deeply as I desire peace and goodness for others, I also believe so do the people who are sitting across the table from me. I wanted to be there for that."

***

It will come as no surprise to you that the Wisconsin group did not reach any consensus regarding abortion itself. The inherent values attached to each side of the issue are too deeply held; too viscerally embedded to allow even a whisper of compromise.

They did, however, reach strong agreement on five peripheral solutions that they believe could help reduce the demand for abortions:

1) Require human development education in schools.

"Topics would include: decision-making and autonomy; setting boundaries and asking for/giving consent; social and emotional skills that support making and acting on informed choices; healthy relationships; intimacy and connection; impacts of pornography; body image; safety, sexual and relational abuse, violence prevention, and rape (including legal repercussions); keeping all students, including those who identify as LGBTQI+, free from harassment, exclusion, and discrimination; internet literacy and the impact of culture, media, and social media; human anatomy; puberty and body changes through the lifespan; the fertility cycle, including ovulation and menstruation; contraception, including how it works, effective use, and benefits and risks; abstinence; STI prevention and treatment; pregnancy and pregnancy loss; and where to find resources on these topics as well as trusted adults at home, school, or in the community with whom to discuss them."

Parents would be free to opt out of any related curriculum.

2) Require notification of all options for pregnant women at pregnancy centers, abortion clinics, and prenatal care providers.

"While participants agree the state should continue to produce an easy-to-understand resource, [we] think it should be more comprehensive than it currently is. Topics should include fetal development; legal options for terminating or continuing a pregnancy, including adoption and resources for adoptive parents; potential physical, financial, and mental health impacts of abortion, pregnancy, adoption, and parenting; safety as it relates to abortion procedures, pregnancy, and giving birth; available supplies and financial and community supports; patient rights and standards of care; and any medical qualifications of providers, staff, and volunteers."

3) Extend postpartum Medicaid from the current six months to twelve months.

"Participants believe access to robust, high-quality, and prompt healthcare throughout one's reproductive life supports family planning and long-term health of parents and children.

"They do not universally support the U.S. healthcare system. However, given that it is the current system, they agree that in addition to extended postpartum care, public and private insurance should cover comprehensive pre- and post-natal care, including doula and midwife care, breast pumps, mental healthcare, and pregnancy loss (miscarriage or stillbirth)."

4) Provide a refundable state child tax credit.

"Many pregnant women/people seeking abortions cite financial reasons and most already have one or more children. The credits help alleviate financial stress by providing support towards current needs."

5) Enact family leave, including foster and adoptive parents.

"Paid family leave improves economic security, keeps parents engaged in the workforce, supports parent and child health and well-being, helps new parents bond with babies and build the foundation for healthy attachment, and enables parents to better seek timely and preventative healthcare for themselves and their children."

Once the group's proposals were finalized, Builders posted them online, inviting anyone with a Wisconsin ZIP code to weigh in, approving or disapproving of each one. Some 20,000 Wisconsinites voted, and all five received overwhelming support: none less than seventy-two percent approval. With no clear front-running issue emerging, the group chose to focus on their twelve-month Medicaid proposal. They are currently lobbying members of the state legislature to bring it to a vote.

***

The Wisconsin Builders project was a rare moment of conviviality between the two sides of the abortion debate, but it was not the first. As recently as 2022, the nationwide reconciliation group Braver Angels sponsored a similar discussion group in Jessamine County, Kentucky. Those participants produced a proposal that looked a lot like the Wisconsin group's call for age-appropriate sex education—but also suggested a remarkably bold program of free, long-acting reversible contraception for Kentucky residents. That proposal was based on a Colorado program that reportedly slashed abortion rates by sixty percent—and teen birth rates by fifty-nine percent.

The granddaddy (or should I say, grandmamma) of attempts to reconcile the sides of the abortion debate is most likely one that convened in 1994, following a series of murders at Brookline, Massachusetts abortion clinics. Appalled by the deadly polarization happening around them, leading figures in both the local pro-life and pro-choice movements risked their reputations by initiating an open-ended series of top-secret, face-to-face meetings.

Those six women were a "who's who" of New England abortion activism: Rev. Anne Fowler, a pro-choice Episcopal priest; Madeline McComish, a retired chemist who headed Massachusetts Citizens for Life; Nicki Gamble, president of the state's Planned Parenthood chapter; Melissa Kogut, executive director of the state National Abortion Rights Action League (NARAL); Barbara Thorp, director of the Boston Archdiocese's Pro-Life Office; and Frances X. Hogan, a lawyer who represented numerous pro-life organizations.

"We went into this," Hogan said in a documentary about the group, "as if we were going to the guillotine."

As would be the case among the Wisconsin abortion panelists thirty years later, the first hurdle for the Massachusetts group was terminology: The abortion rights proponents balked at calling the other women "Pro-Life," believing they, too, were in the business of preserving lives. One side preferred the term "fetus" while the other insisted on "unborn baby." They finally, reluctantly, settled on "human fetus."

They could not even agree on the significance of the Declaration of Independence: The pro-life side read its claim to a right to life as affirmation of the unborn's personhood; the pro-choice side insisted the right to life and liberty clearly prioritizes the notion of a woman's right to choose.

Predictably, six years of clandestine meetings yielded no agreement on the issue of abortion. Indeed, the only real "breakthrough" the members seem to recall is the realization, some two years in, that they would never, ever come to even the most tangential compromise.

But by that time, something truly enduring had taken root: A sense of not only shared humanity, but actual friendship. The women began keeping track of each other's birthdays and other important dates. They celebrated good times and mourned collectively over the sad ones.

In the end, the women walked away acknowledging two unshakable values: One regarding their unchanged views on abortion; the other regarding the immutable nature of friendship.

"When we face our opponent, we see her dignity and goodness," the women jointly wrote in the 2021 Boston Globe article that revealed their six-year journey. "We have learned to avoid being overreactive and disparaging to the other side and to focus instead on affirming our respective causes."

Most improbably, Nichols later said, "We became friends, strange as though that seems even to me. It changed my life."

No current issue cuts more deeply to the heart of the American soul than abortion, a matter of irreconcilable differences that all too easily erupts into open conflict. Heading for my next stop, watching the lake-dotted landscape of Wisconsin slide beneath my airliner window, I breathe a prayer of thanks for those who embark on the seemingly thankless endeavor of finding a fragment of common cause and then moving on, occasionally glancing at those across the divide, smiling faintly, and wrapping each other in a compassionate embrace.

Pyramid Lake

Alberta, Canada: Apart Together

A Side Trip to Jasper, and America's Possible Future

As a kid, I believed travel could never get more exotic than going to Canada. Each summer, my dad loaded up the Country Squire station wagon, pointed that powerful V-8 engine north, and drove us up, up, up the New York Thruway and across the Thousand Island Bridge. (My brothers and sisters and I would stretch our toes forward, under the front bench seat, trying to be the first to cross the international border.)

Most of our two weeks were spent swimming in the barely defrosted waters of Thirty Island Lake, north of Kingston, Ontario. But occasionally we'd venture to Ottawa, and most spectacularly, in 1967, to the world's fair in Montreal where—and I'm not sure everyone knows this—most of the people speak French!

Besides being, like, a whole other country, where they measure distance in meters and still have some vaguely defined/rock solid relationship to the King of England, it turns out Canada has been dealing with existential issues for about as long as there's been Canada; issues that seem as un-solvable—and maybe even more so—than the ones that plague us, as they say, "downstairs in the States." Yet despite schisms that have led to name calling, threats of secession and even occasional bomb throwing (the literal type), you'd be hard-pressed to find a Canadian who does not identify, proudly and loudly, as a Canuck (as we call them).

I do believe I mentioned earlier that one of my day jobs is as a travel writer, and I was in the middle of working on this book when I was invited to experience, on behalf of my readers, the considerable wonders of Alberta—specifically, Calgary, Banff and Jasper. And it hit me: Why not take a slight detour north from my U.S. loop and pick the brains of some actual Canadians regarding the ways in which Canadians, in the face of insurmountable differences, still manage to relate to each other?

I headed west over MichConsin, turned right at Montana, and plunged into the exotic wilds of Canada's plains provinces. Oh, Canada, maybe you have some answers for us.

***

From Calgary, the last outpost on Canada's Great Plain, I drive northwest, into the heart of the Canadian Rockies. The trip from Calgary to Jasper is among the world's most dramatically beautiful; past lakes that launch seasonal regattas of freshwater icebergs; through valleys framed by rugged, snow-topped peaks; directly beneath North America's one and only drive-up glacier.

My northern trek ends at Jasper's Pyramid Lake Lodge, on a low hill overlooking startlingly clear Pyramid Lake, which, on a calm day like this, reflects on its mirror-like surface the hulking mass of Pyramid Mountain.

That's a lot of pyramids for one Rocky Mountain locale, but the notion of a four-sided structure ascending to a singular point could be considered an illustration of Canada's segmented political state. Canada's nationwide federal government is composed primarily of representatives from four parties: The center-left Liberal Party, the center-right Conservative Party, the French-Canadian Bloc Quebecois Party, and the far-left New Democratic Party. (The relatively tiny Green Party is an emerging force in the country, but to include it here would totally ruin my pyramid scheme.)

The Liberals and Conservatives are a decent analog for our Democrats and Republicans, historically jockeying for primacy in the country's parliament, and for the right to select the nation's Prime Minister. The New Democratic Party has regional strengths, but for decades, the real wild card has been the Quebecois group—based almost exclusively in the French-speaking regions of Quebec Province—who have long agitated to split from the rest of Canada and establish their own North American *Isle de France.*

That may sound somewhat familiar to Americans who periodically hear rumblings of secession from residents of their more conservative states, particularly Texas (which, conspiracy theorists suspect, is a big reason why it's the only state with its own, self-supporting power grid). But while the U.S. separatists base their beef largely on policy differences with the Washington, DC "swamp," secession-minded French Canadians primarily see themselves as a culture set apart from their English-speaking countrymen, with not enough common touchstones to justify national unity.

Here in Canada's west, though, there are secession tremors of an entirely different nature; ones that more resemble the societal split now shaking up life in their neighbors to the south. There is a reason they call Alberta "Canada's Texas:" The Athabasca Oil Sands, which sprawl across most of Alberta's northeastern quarter, are, by far, the nation's greatest source of export wealth. Add to that the province's centuries-long history of cattle ranching and it's easy to imagine J.R. Ewing scheming his next diabolical move from, instead of Dallas, some tower in downtown Calgary. (Yes, nearly every major star from the 1980s prime time soap "Dallas" is long gone, but if you've got a more contemporary Big D cultural reference, you're welcome to it.)

Like Texas, Alberta is also historically more conservative than the country's coastal liberal bastions, and in recent years a familiar refrain has begun to blow down from the Rockies and across the plain: "Why should those East-and-West Liberals dictate our lives?"

I'd put the question to a red-bearded fellow named Tim at, appropriately, a Tim Horton's coffee shop in Calgary's Dominion Centre. Looking me in the eye, Tim thoughtfully removed his Massey Ferguson ball cap and scratched his head.

"I've got nothing against the people out there," he said, pointing in the general direction of the Atlantic Ocean, 3,000 miles away. "Good people. But I'm tired of feeding them and putting gas in their cars and all I get back from them is stuff like 'You're trying to kill the planet."

He picked up his Tim Horton cinnamon roll, as if to take a bite, then stopped.

"The planet, can you believe that?" he snickered. "They wouldn't know a cow pie if they stepped in it."

Tim stopped short of calling for Alberta to take a walk from the rest of Canada. He said he loves being a Canadian. He just wants to be *his* kind of Canadian, and doesn't think that's too much to ask.

At this writing, of Alberta's thirty-seven federal election districts, thirty-one are considered safe, likely, or leaning Conservative. Most conservative of all is the swath of Alberta that stretches from the foothills of the Rocky

Chloe MacEachern

Mountains east toward Saskatchewan, which shares Alberta's conservative tendencies, but with only about one-quarter the population clout. In sheer numbers, these conservative provinces—two out of ten—are dramatically outnumbered by voters in the rest of the country. But their natural resources and strategic location between the liberal east and west give them outsized influence.

***

I am admiring my Brussels Caesar salad at Aalto, the big-windowed restaurant at Pyramid Lake Lodge. I don't know how you feel about Brussels sprouts, but the rising aroma of anchovy gremolata, gruyere cheese and smoked pork belly has me seriously considering the benefits of Canadian citizenship.

My dinner companions—both on the same travel press trip with me—are Chloe MacEachern, in her early twenties, from Calgary, and Alice, closer to middle age, a French Canadian from Quebec. Alice has asked me not to use her real name, since she's a recognizable media figure and doesn't feel comfortable talking national politics. Chloe, on the other hand, seems to delight in talking on the record about all things Canadian. Both have thought a lot about where their country is heading.

"We need to get one thing clear," Chloe begins. "Some people in Alberta may want to leave Canada, but they absolutely do *not* want to become the fifty-first state."

It's an important distinction to make speaking to an American, who in recent times has heard his president repeatedly insist that Canada—or parts of Canada—would be a nice fit for an extra star or two on the flag.

"Still, there are a lot of people who value being an Albertan over being a Canadian," she continues. "And what that means is there is some sentiment for Alberta to become its own country."

Alberta's main beef (that's a commodity joke) is the perception that the Canadian federal government is more concerned with caring for people its main population centers—the East and West—than with those who are more spread out.

"The East has all those more liberal people and, like, *nobody* lives here," says Chloe. "The people out here say, 'Those people in the East don't listen to us. They don't respect us. Who needs 'em?'"

The sentiment is so intense that, just a few months after we are speaking, Alberta will hold a referendum on separating from the rest of Canda. Of course, any such vote is a strictly aspirational one: Just about everyone understands that Alberta will depart from Canada no sooner than Earth separates from the Solar System.

"The rest of Canada would have to agree," says Chloe. "And that's not going to happen, if only because we are the nation's cash cow. Plus, even with our resources we couldn't afford it. We don't have a currency. And the First Nations, who make up a huge part of the province, would never go along with it."

This simmering desire to depart the rest of the country—which Chloe believes has been made more acute by Canadians' observations of divisions in the United States—can't help but eat at the fabric of the Canadian federation. But then again, the notion of secession is nothing new in the country's eastern half, where French Canadians have toyed with the notion of a separate country for a good, long time: Quebec has held referendums on separation twice, in 1980 and 1995. The measure failed both times—by a thin margin the second time around. In 1996, the country's Supreme Court actually laid out the ground rules for any province that was considering secession—importantly, ruling that under certain circumstances, a province could, indeed, go its own way.

"We're not French, but we're not really Canadian because we speak French," says Alice, who speaks English with a musical French lilt. "We're some kind of entity all our own. It's why so many people keep coming back to the idea of being separated."

Then again, like most feuding families, while French Canadians don't mind bickering over the dinner table, they don't necessarily appreciate outside interlopers: Alice tells me that recent US overtures to making Canada the fifty-first state have, against all expectations, galvanized French Canadians in favor of remaining one country.

"Québécois have never been more Canadian than they are now," she says.

Chloe laughs.

"I would say events in the United States have brought out the opposite sentiment in Alberta," Chloe observes. "A lot of people are looking at what's happening in the U.S. and saying, 'Yeah, I want a part of that.'"

At least, I say, Canada is not enduring a crushing, US-style conflict over immigration.

Chloe and Alice look at each other, seemingly both amused and aghast.

"Immigration is the BIG thing," says Chloe. "For example, we have students who come to Canada on student visas and that's interfering with the job market for Canadian students."

"It's very challenging on so many levels," continues Alice. "We've always been this very welcoming country; it's one thing that defines us. And we need immigrants to fill jobs."

This is all sounding vaguely familiar.

"But," she continues, "they opened up the country a little too much. We ended up with too many immigrants. It made me angry with the government, and it made me angry with the immigrants."

Now its sounding *very* familiar.

Part of Canada's continuing problem, Chloe suggests, may be that it has not historically considered itself a melting pot.

"The difference, as I see it, is when people go to the States, they want to become Americans," says Chloe. "They want what America has to offer; the American Dream.

"People come to Canada simply because they can. They see this as a good place to land; a safe place to land. And unlike Americans, they want to maintain, at least to some degree, the identity of where they came from. That's why Canadians tend to maintain pockets of community."

For French Canadians, Alice adds, that can be a daily struggle.

"We are French people surrounded by the English," she says. "So, our life is fighting to keep what's left of our French-ness alive. We were colonized here by the French, then organized by the English. We're too French to be North Americans and too North American to be French. Even today, there are so many things we don't understand about Canadian, English, and American culture. For many French Canadians, it's like being trapped. We'll fight that feeling until we die."

***

Dessert has arrived. We've decided, as a demonstration of unity, to share the crème caramel and pavlova with Saskatoon berry curd.

As our spoons jockey for position, I'm struck that Canada has been dealing for so long with seemingly unsurmountable—occasionally violent—divisions, yet has projected to the world a sense of benign unity that consistently earns it recognition, depending on the survey you read, as among world's top dozen or so countries to live in. (The U.S., by comparison, almost never noses its way into the top ten.)

And so, I pop my dessert question: It does not appear Canada's divisions are any more severe than those in the US, and they've been percolating for a long time. What keeps Canadians together?

"Celine Dion," says Alice.

"Hockey," says Chloe.

My spoonful of crème brûlée hovers near my mouth, squiggling in surprise.

"Really?" I splutter. "Isn't that a little, I don't know, superficial?"

In unison, the two raise their eyes to the restaurant's vaulted ceiling in exasperation.

"A country defines itself by its culture," says Alice. "Celine is an example, but we have many, many cultural things like that that connect us. As I said, French is what defines me. The French language, in particular. But it's not just me: All across Canada there are small French communities. We share that language; we're united by it, and by our shared history."

"Hockey makes me so freaking patriotic," Chloe exclaims. "I watch the seventeen or eighteen-year-olds play in the World Juniors, and I'm like, 'That's my boys!' Did you watch the Four Nations Tournament earlier this year?"

I shake my head as if to say, "Sorry, I missed it this time around," but in fact, I've never heard of the Four Nations Tournament.

"Canada, Sweden, Finland, and the States," she says. "The Gold Medal game was Canada versus the U.S. This was February. Right in the middle of the fifty-first state' stuff, yeah? It was incredible. No one ate dinner that night. They just watched the game.

"And when Canada won that game, well, if you want to talk about what can unite an Eastern Liberal with a Western Conservative, it was that weekend of hockey."

"I remember exactly what you're talking about," adds Alice. "I don't like hockey at all. But you could feel it. You could feel it everywhere."

Now Chloe can't stop talking about it.

"I mean, if the United States wanted to invade Canada, there is nothing we could do about it. But in hockey, HA! We own you!"

***

We rise from our table and make our way across the restaurant. At one table after another, diners glance up from their plates, smile, and nod. I've never seen anything quite like it.

I mention it to Chloe, and she suggests I've stumbled upon another unifying quality of Canadians.

"We're *nice*," she says. "You always hear about that stereotype of the nice, polite Canadian. And I think it's true. If I had a flat tire in a car with a Liberal Party bumper sticker, I have no doubt that someone passing by with a 'Fuck Trudeau' flag would not think twice about stopping to help me.

"We have that fundamental sense of community. I think that is very Canadian."

Could it also be American, I wonder? As Americans fret about their country's future, are they judging fellow citizens based on their generous hearts, or on their poisonous social media feeds?

It's after ten p.m., but here in the Canadian Rockies, the sky is still bright as we exit to the parking lot.

My hopes for America are brighter as well. Here is Canada, where entire populations have actually voted to leave the country, where there is not even pretense of cultural assimilation, where immigration, energy, and political divides are a daily trial…and where a segment of the country is emphatically all-in for a north-of-the-border MAGA movement.

And yet here are the Canadians, smiling up from their tables, sitting on Adirondack chairs on a dock jutting into the darkening waters of Pyramid Lake, listening to Celine Dion and cheering on their hockey teams.

And being nice.

Americans are nice, too, I affirm to myself. I have no doubt whatsoever that the Interstate Highway System is teeming with motorists who, seeing my car pulled over with a bumper sticker that on Facebook would draw from them a spitting insult, would not hesitate to pull over and help. I consider the mounting number of recent U.S. natural disasters, and how the endless caravans of aid, the GoFundMe campaigns, the armies of volunteers never seem to come on the condition of party affiliation (in contrast to their elected officials, most of whom seem determined to blame earthquakes, fires, and floods not on nature, but on their political opposites).

Is the United States headed for a Canadian future, one of balkanized populations engaged in an occasional dance of departure, whose gaping political and cultural wounds are largely bound by bandages of mass entertainment, pivotal sporting events, and perceived common antagonists? Are compassionate grassroot responses to an occasional natural calamity enough to sustain a national sense of emotional connection? That all sounds like a tenuously superficial way for a nation to survive, but it seems to work for our neighbors up north.

A friend in Toronto once told me, "We Canadians think of ourselves as living on the second floor, and the folks downstairs are having a nervous breakdown."

I'm left to wonder if America's post-breakdown personality will absorb the positive lessons of Canada's survival.

Maybe our common niceness will save us. Maybe, in a way, we could become the eleventh province.

Rocky Mountain Field Institute at work

Colorado: Where the Trails Converge

Companies and Conservationists Take a Walk on the Wild Side

The Colorado sun is brilliant, and the sky is the same gemlike blue I've just left behind in the Canadian Rockies; the kind you only get when you're a mile or so above sea level. But on this February weekend the temperature will not climb beyond the mid-thirties.

Bundled against the cold in blue hooded sweatshirts and thick work gloves, four men are carrying a litter up a steep length of the Lori Cohen Memorial 5k trail—an easy-to-reach and popular path that rises into the Rocky Mountain foothills near Colorado Springs.

Each guy takes one end of a pole, the litter's leather straps cradling not an injured human, but a rock the size of a small suitcase.

The volunteers' destination is a sharp switchback on the trail ahead; a spot where erosion threatens to wash the trail away. The solution to prevent further erosion, of course: Lug several tons of rocks up here to create a retaining wall. But there's no way to maneuver heavy machinery on the narrow, winding course. For these men on this chilled Saturday morning, lugging rocks in a sling, it may as well be the Stone Age.

Weeks later, this same trail is spotted with women clearing debris and

Sam Hinkle

loose rocks. They trim back whatever Gambel oak branches have not already been nibbled away by deer and turkeys.

Trudging this trail, lugging rocks and clipping vegetation, the men and women talk about the moment-to-moment changes in Colorado's ever-shifting weather. They chat regarding strategies to limit wear and tear on Colorado's well-traveled trails. They discuss the distribution of weight in their packs and the location of fresh water and the best way to approach a wayward prickly pear cactus.

What they do not talk about…almost ever…is politics.

That, I learn a few weeks later, is completely by design.

"We don't talk with our volunteers about politics…at all," says Sam Hinkle, development director for the Rocky Mountain Field Institute, which sponsored both volunteer projects.

"That would be inherently counterproductive to the work we're trying to get done."

Sam is showing me around the headquarters of RMFI, a modest office space on the outskirts of Colorado Springs, a short drive from the Rockies' foothills. Were I to exit the parking lot outside and drive to a clearing up the street, I'd have a pretty good view of Pike's Peak.

"I'm not saying those discussions don't happen among our volunteers and staff people," he hastens to add, "but debating politics is not part of our mission. Our mission is action; caring for these wild places that all of us share, no matter what our politics are."

Sam—bright-eyed, endlessly enthusiastic and clearly wishing he were outside hiking rather than hunkering down here with some writer—grew up here in Colorado Springs. Hiking the hills and canyons of the Front Range, he always felt he was close to the land. Only when he went to study at Whitman College in Walla Walla, Washington did he come to realize he'd merely been scratching the terrain's red-soiled surface.

"I had a professor," he recalls, "who affixed a Wi-Fi satellite dish on top of a horse trailer, and we just drove through the American West."

His eyes sparkling at the memory, Sam recalls a stop in Moab, Utah, as the moment when he began to understand the many different ways people of all political and social strata approach the natural world.

"There are literally hundreds of user groups who make use of Moab," he says. "Climbing, running, biking, RV-ing, of course. But also, there's the extractive industry; all the big companies and workers who are mining and lumbering out there."

Superficially, it would seem those who look at the natural environment as a recreational or ecological resource and those who commercially exploit the land and its plant life for large-scale harvesting face irreconcilable differences. That's how Sam felt—until he considered the words of a retired woman he met in Moab, traveling the country with her husband in their RV.

"The reason we're here," she told him, "is that the outdoors are an arena for all of us to be together without conflict."

"Listening to her," he recalls, "I started to feel like I'd been a little naive. Because here I was documenting all the conflicts over these public lands, and this woman understood that the outdoors represents an opportunity for us to figure out how to live as a community."

Nature lovers who take a big picture view of nature, Sam believes, are more likely to find kinship with those who look at the natural world with a different sense of priorities.

"There are a lot of overlapping desires for how to use the landscape," he says. "We all do different things in the outdoors. Some of us hike or bike; some of us make a living helping other people hike or bike. And then there are people for whom the removal of timber, the extraction of mined resources, are their livelihood.

"For all those people, the preservation of the natural landscape is in their shared best interest, no matter what their political background."

Sam leads me out back, to the RMFI's storage room/loading dock. Stacked in a jumbled sort of order are pieces of trail maintenance equipment required for an upcoming week-plus expedition into Colorado's high country: picks and shovels, propane tanks and heaters, water jugs and dehydrated food.

All of this will be transported miles into the wilderness by teams of up to thirty volunteers.

It's easy to imagine a platoon of tree-hugging liberals trudging off into the mountains on another quixotic crusade in defense of Mother Earth. But to do so would deny the wide swath true environmentalism cuts through American culture.

Essential to much of what RMFI accomplishes each year is due in no small part to groups like the Colorado Motorcycle Trail Riders Association (CMTRA), which, after a quick survey of its Facebook page followers, proves to be no bastion of liberal wokeness.

"All of our trail work is done by hand," says Sam. "Groups like the Motorcycle Trail Riders transport a lot of our equipment and staff. They donate their time and their expertise, and they save us thousands of dollars a year."

Especially since the days of COVID-19—when just about the only public place people felt safe was out in nature—corporations have learned the dollars-and-cents value of protecting the environment, according to Hinkle.

"The outdoor industry cannot exist without the outdoors," he shrugs. "And for the outdoors to continue to exist, people need to take care of it. It needs stewards—especially corporate stewards who have financial resources to pour into it."

Outdoor recreation is, it turns out, big business, accounting for something like 2.3 percent of America's Gross Domestic Product, Sam says. What's more, the sector's annual growth regularly outpaces the nation's GDP in general. He explains that in the Pike's Peak region alone, sales taxes collected from visitors are essential to fund local governments, and over the past few years property values have grown by some $585 million simply because so many people want to live near the area's public lands.

Often, Sam says, two interest groups will come around to the exact same environmentally friendly cause precisely because of their differing perspectives. An example is the case of the greenback cutthroat trout, a palm-sized, extremely threatened species—and a favorite of fly fishers—with just one major remaining refuge: Bear Creek, in the foothills above Colorado Springs.

Environmentalists want to preserve the fish primarily because that's what environmentalists do: post "Stop" signs at the cliffs of extinction over which far too many animal species tumble. Corporate interests want to keep the greenback cutthroat trout alive for a considerably more mercenary—yet no less legitimate—reason: To draw sport fishers who want a photo of themselves having hooked one (before throwing it back, of course).

"They're looking at it through very different lenses," Sam says, "but they're caring for this place together."

Hinkle's main job is raising funds for RMFI, so I put to him a simple question: Say you're approaching a straight-up, traditionally conservative corporate entity about preserving, say a kind of antelope. How would that approach differ from the pitch you'd present to a century-old environmental foundation, seeking money for the same project?

Immediately, I can see the wheels turning behind Sam's eyes.

"Well, you talk about the impact that overlaps their interests, right?" he says. "If it's a business, I'm going to talk business with them. If you're a tech business that's looking to draw experienced coders from elsewhere in the country to Colorado Springs, you know you're not going to be able to offer them, you know, a San Francisco salary."

But he can offer them a lot of things San Francisco can't: A chance to go mountain biking after work. A lunch hour sitting among the red rock splendor of Garden of the Gods, which is just a few minutes from downtown Colorado Springs. He can talk to them about how developing the natural environment also develops a workforce that pays the taxes that provide millions of dollars for teachers' salaries, firefighters, nurses—the backbones of society.

Pitching an environmental group, on the other hand, involves magnification of what they probably already see as their mission statement.

"For them," he says, "the sell is that environmental piece: We all exist on the land. We all need to preserve the land."

While Colorado's Front Range is generally considered a progressive stronghold, Colorado Springs is by far the most conservative city in the state—and by some measures the entire country: It's surrounded by military bases, and home to some of the nation's most conservative faith-based groups, including James Dobson's Focus on the Family and The Navigators (whose headquarters, located in a century-old castle nestled deep in a red rock canyon, offers one of the prettiest drives in the foothills).

"So, there's a real mix," says Sam, and his voice rises at the excitement of the challenge. "But no matter who you are, regardless of what walk of life you're on, you and everyone else are going to gather in the outdoors.

"Our goal is to make sure that we all can continue to do so. Not just our generation, but the next seven generations."

Sam's words hang in the air for a moment or two. Somewhere in a nearby office, a coffee machine is gently percolating.

"Did that answer your question?" he finally asks. "I feel like I ramble sometimes."

He doesn't notice me reaching for my wallet. Sign me up.

***

That afternoon, I resolved to visit Bear Creek, home to those endangered but universally beloved greenback cutthroat trout. I cross a rustic wooden footbridge spanning the creek and ascend the reasonably steep slope of the Cub Trail. Less than four miles from the four-lane scar that Interstate 25 carves into the foothills through Colorado Springs, the air is fresh with the scent of pine and alive with the coos of mourning doves and the Chihuahua-like bark of northern flickers.

Trudging up a medium slope, watching my black shoes assume the color of the red-dusted trail, I'm gradually aware of two competing sounds fading into my consciousness: From uphill, the unmistakable crunch and click of a mountain bike, advancing at a pretty decent clip. From below, the rapidly approaching chatter of two or more hikers, clearly intent on covering a lot more ground than I will.

As so often happens on narrow byways, we all meet up on the same spot at the same moment. The yellow-helmeted, goggled biker slides to a stop, raising a cloud of red dirt and barely remaining upright. The hikers, a couple older than even me, rear back on their heels, startled and wide-eyed. (As for me, having sensed the coming encounter, I'm one step off trail, assuming my accustomed role as a trying-to-be-invisible observer.)

Now, I've been around people my age and older long enough to know what's going to happen next: "Hey, kid! Slow down! You'll kill someone!" Also, "You guys need to stay to your side of the trail!"

But that's not what happens.

"Nice stop!" laughs the woman hiker. "I don't think I would have been able to do that!"

"I didn't see you coming," the biker apologizes. "Sorry."

"See anything?" the woman asks, pointing uphill.

"I might have seen a squirrel," he says. "Maybe a chipmunk. I really just mostly look straight ahead..."

"Ha! Of course!" says the man hiker. "Beautiful day."

"Beautiful day!" says the woman.

"Yeah," says the biker.

All three turn to me, standing there, grinning like a dope.

"Hello!" they say, more or less in unison.
And then they are off, chatting, pedaling, separately and together.

Christmas at the Mine Shaft

Madrid, New Mexico: A Table at the Mine Shaft Tavern

It Helps to Think Everyone is a Little Bit Crazy

In the high desert village of Madrid, New Mexico, floating coal dust dirties your clothes even when you're standing still. There's no cell phone service. Many homes still have outhouses. And the drinking water smells like Hell, literally: Every glass stinks of sulfur from the coal mine-honeycombed aquifer below.

Despite all that—or maybe because of it—"I wouldn't live anywhere else," says Barbara Fail.

The five-hour drive due south of Colorado Springs—skirting the Rockies' Front Range, crossing the Santa Fe Trail at the rubble of Fort Union National Monument, passing through Las Vegas (not *that* Las Vegas, but the picturesque cow town where Tom Mix made many of his movies)—has landed me here next to Barbara, who first visited Madrid as a twenty-something hippie. For the forty ensuing years, she tells me, flashing a sly smile that evokes that long-ago Flower Child, "I knew I wanted to come back here."

Around 2010, while running an art gallery in Manhattan, she decided to make the move at last. She opened a studio on Madrid's main street and ran it until she retired a few years ago. Now, Barbara says, she's here to stay.

Barbara Fail & Les Reasonover on the Mine Shaft porch

"I laugh when people say Madrid is a hard place to live," she says. "For me, this is the easiest place in the world. Everyone gets to be themselves. You can live off the grid. People take care of each other. It's great."

We're at a table just a few feet from the long wooden bar at the Mine Shaft Tavern, the social center for most of the 300 or so folks who live within Madrid's 300 acres. The original Mine Shaft burned down on Christmas Day, 1944. When the replacement opened in 1947, that extended wooden bar was hailed as "The Longest in New Mexico." It may still be. No one seems particularly motivated to canvas the rest of the state's watering holes to update the data.

"You'll notice there's no seats at that bar," says Les Reasonover, Barbara's partner for over a decade, who's joined us. "That's because the coal miners who came in here after work had been bent over all day down in the shafts. All they wanted in the evening was to stand up straight and have a drink."

Les moved here in the early 2010s after a career at Sandia National Laboratories in nearby Albuquerque, designing microscopic machines for national security applications. His gray beard frames an easy smile, and long hair hangs far beyond his shoulders from beneath a cream-colored cowboy hat.

"I'd always thought I'd like to live here sometime," he says. "Then I broke my back in a motorcycle accident. Now I'm getting paid not to work, and Madrid is a great place to do that."

This is my fourth visit to Madrid. The first time was purely serendipitous; a random stop in 2013 when my wife, Carolyn, and I took a decidedly itinerary-less drive around the American southwest. We were heading north on Route 14—also known as the Turquoise Trail, after the blue-green stone once mined in this area by early Pueblo people—when the road suddenly widened at this ramshackle array of shops, yard sculptures, and painted picket fences.

I returned a couple of years later to write about the place as an off-beat—and largely forbidding—retirement destination. Then, while in New Mexico working on a 2021 piece about the state's nuclear weapons history, I drove a hundred miles or so out of my way just to sit on the Mine Shaft porch and watch the sun set beyond the round-topped hills.

This time, I'm here with a purpose: To explore Madrid, with its median age of 59.6, as a template for a community that seems to not just sustain itself, but positively thrive as a population of wildly differing political and social views. Madrid, I've always felt, not only celebrates itself as a place where people are comfortable in their own skin, but where they're equally comfortable letting other people live in theirs.

At the heart of Madrid, where Route 14 winds its rolling course through the Cerrillos Hills, stand rustic old mining town houses now converted into art galleries and restaurants, catering to tourists who drive up from Albuquerque or down from Santa Fe, thirty miles to the north. A block or so off the main road spreads a grid of dirt streets with names like Old Goat and Back Road. Out here, the houses become markedly less kept-up, with sloping roofs and dilapidated porches—yet most are adorned with works of art, either outdoor murals or statuary ranging from abstract shapes made of concrete to assemblages of old wood and machine parts. These houses appear to be occupied largely by artists and gallery owners.

Farther out still are frame structures that seem supported by little more than ornery stubbornness, separated by vast stretches of scrub-marked wilderness. This, I was told on an earlier visit, is where you'll find Madrid's most dedicated individualists; folks who have receded from society with a vengeance. Historically, most of them were disaffected Vietnam War veterans. Only a few of those original veterans remain, but they've given way to similarly reclusive vets of America's various early twenty-first century Middle East conflicts. Visitors are warned not to venture out there, lest they end up facing the business end of a rifle.

In recent years, on large parcels outside of town—at times a stone's throw from the ramshackle homes of those resident outsiders—folks from the cities have started building beautiful adobe houses with floor-to-ceiling windows and hot tubs.

One such home, on a bluff overlooking town, has been sarcastically dubbed "The Castle" by locals.

The nexus of it is the Mine Shaft, where the camo-wearing recluse, the consignment-conscious gallery owner and the slumming crypto bro will all eventually drop in to kick back with a drink and hear some music.

The table at which I am seated with Barbara and Les has several empty chairs; a strategic choice to encourage tonight's drop-ins to set a spell. Barbara keeps apologizing because it's Tuesday, the slowest night of the week. Had I come tomorrow, the place would have been hopping with the music of Cactus Slim and the Goat Heads, a beloved local group I got to experience on my second visit here.

But I'm grateful for the relative peace and quiet of bar conversations and a steady soundtrack of recorded country music. I'm here for the talk.

***

Anyone who arrives in Madrid pronouncing the town's name like that city in Spain will quickly be corrected.

"It's MAD-rid," a bearded local told me shortly after my first arrival at the Mine Shaft. "Emphasis on the 'mad!'"

The fact is that about 130 years ago, when the place was willed into existence by a coal company to house miners and support staff, Madrid was pronounced the traditional way. Among the West's earliest electrified cities (Thomas Edison helped build a power plant here in 1900), it was one of New Mexico's most bustling locales, known nationwide for its annual display of 150,000 Christmas lights and for having the first lit ball field west of the Mississippi. (The field is still there, and lights still hang from perilously tall and slender telephone poles.)

There's a story about Walt Disney and Madrid that is almost certainly apocryphal, but which hints at the universality of the town's appealing weirdness: On a cross-country flight in the 1930's, while coming in for a night landing in Albuquerque, Walt and his companion, animator Walter Lantz (creator of Woody Woodpecker) saw through their airliner windows the streets of Madrid at Christmas, its colorful grid lit like a wild abstract painting against the pitch-black landscape. Fascinated, the pair headed up to Madrid the next day to investigate.

Disney never forgot the sight, urban legend says, and he used it as inspiration for lighting his Disneyland theme park—rising, Madrid-like, from acres of Southern California orange groves.

So, is Madrid, New Mexico, the original Magic Kingdom? That notion might dismay current enthusiasts of both institutions, but if anyone ever had an eye for concepts that appealed across the American social spectrum, it was the creator of Mickey Mouse.

The crash came in the 1950s, when the coal mine closed and the populace fled Madrid like tumbleweeds blown by a high desert windstorm. For more than twenty years, Madrid stood virtually empty, a destination for adventurous photographers and a curiosity to motorists passing through.

The land remained under the ownership of the mining company's former superintendent, and in the early 1970s his son began to rent the old houses for a few dollars a month and later to sell them dirt cheap. The offer primarily attracted two wildly different groups: socially disaffected Vietnam War veterans and free-spirited craftspeople and artists, largely from San Francisco, Chicago, and nearby Santa Fe.

"I knew a few guys from that original generation," says Les. "And they all told me the same story: Back in the early '70s, all these people started to show up. The hippies, the gays, the lesbians, the artists—and there was a lot of disparity between them and the Vietnam War vets who'd been here."

As he leans back in his wooden chair and relates the story of Madrid's defining moment, Les reminds me of a high school history teacher I once had; a guy who never lost his sense of wonder regarding the creation of the Declaration of Independence.

"One day," he says, "they all had a meeting—right outside of here, in the Mine Shaft parking lot. And they said, 'What are we going to do?'

"Well, they came to an agreement. There would be one rule: Do No Harm. Don't hurt anybody, whatever else you do. Whatever drug you do, we don't care. Whatever your sexuality is, we don't care.

"You hurt somebody, and you'll get a rap. But if you don't hurt anybody, it's all cool."

That vibe, Les says, has informed Madrid's culture for nearly sixty years.

"Sometimes," he adds, "I have to take the young guys aside and remind them of it. And they get it."

One spiritual descendant of that first Madrid generation is Jesse Gayle, a thirty-something, dark-haired musician who suggests to me a grown-up Wednesday from The Addams Family. She's been waved over to our table by Barbara. "When it comes to different types, we've got everybody here," Jesse says. "I mean, you want to talk about politics? I know people here who believe in Reptilians (shape-shifting reptile-like aliens who control Earth). We've got Super Democrats and Super Republicans. Some people hate guns and a lot of us carry them. But what difference does all that make? We gotta get along, right?"

"Oh, here's Bill!" Barbara exclaims, pulling a chair away from the table. "Bill's been here forever!"

"Forever," it turns out, is about fifty years. Bill Hogrebe, at the time a troubled twenty-two-year-old escaping family troubles in St. Louis, happened upon Madrid right when the old mining houses were being rented for nearly nothing. He snapped one up—first living in a place on the main street and then, more than forty years ago, settling in at what was once the town icehouse. He's been there ever since. And he still hasn't installed indoor plumbing.

Bill sits down with us. Tall and thin with a wry smile and a voice like Sam Elliott, he looks around the Mine Shaft and nods nostalgically.

"This was my bar in the old days," he says. "This was the place to go. Really, the *only* place to go."

Bill and his buddies—military veterans and drifters similarly uneasy with the world beyond New Mexico's high desert—regularly closed The Mine Shaft after last call. But as Madrid began to draw artists and their customers, Bill's circle retreated from the town's mainstream.

Aside from emerging each morning to go to work as a private health care provider in and around Santa Fe, he says, "I pretty much stayed home for twenty years."

Locals gather at the Mine Shaft

Les can attest to that. For years, he says, he'd try to engage Bill in conversation.

"I'd see Bill heading for his mailbox, and I'd yell 'Hey!'" Les recalls. "But he'd just keep looking straight down and then head back to his house."

Bill smiles softly and nods.

"Then," Bill says, "about a year ago, I realized my friends had all died. I was just sitting alone in my house smoking a joint, and I said to myself, 'This ain't gonna be my life.'"

So now, most nights, you'll find Bill sauntering down to the Mine Shaft, hanging with people like Barbara the former Manhattan art dealer and Les the retired national security engineer.

"When I first came back," Bill recalls, "a lot of people didn't even know who I was."

He points to a far corner of the tavern.

"But I sat right over there every night, quietly, and I mumbled to myself, 'These people don't know it, but *this is my fucking bar*.'"

"Hey, Bill," says Les, "are you carrying tonight?"

"Of course," Bill answers, and naturally I assume this is gun talk. It seems like nearly everyone here—liberal, conservative, and in-between—has at least one gun, and probably lots more than that. But then Bill reaches under his shirt and pulls out not a Colt 45, but two honest-to-goodness chirping parakeets. The birds seem happy to be out in fresh air. They hop onto a short walking stick Bill's been carrying.

"Just two?" asks Les. He turns to me. "Sometimes he's got eight of 'em."

Bill shrugs.

"Whattya gonna do? Gotta take the birds for a walk."

***

Besides Bill, it is still possible to spot members of that first wave of Madroids, as the locals call themselves. But their numbers are diminishing as age and hard living catch up with them, and their numbers are subsumed by a continuing trickle of newcomers, inexplicably drawn by the town's unique mixture of high culture and low standard of living.

My first morning in Madrid, one cool spring day in 2016, I sat at a table outside Java Junction—the town's primo coffee shop—near a klatch of bearded Vets in M.I.A. baseball caps, bandanas and denim jackets, the men downed their piping hot coffee alarmingly fast and smoked with careless abandon.

I introduced myself, and was somehow not surprised by the response I got.

"A writer, eh?" said a vet named Ron, not unpleasantly. "The last writer we had here we ran out of town." Two companions at his table nodded solemnly.

That's a common sentiment among the Madrid's veterans community; visiting writers often paint them as something of a cross between Rambo and Grizzly Adams, an easy generalization that doesn't come close to portraying the complexities of their community. Here at Java Junction, Ron and two other vets; a Vietnam era contemporary named Mark and a younger man named James, alternately insulted each other, slapped each other's backs, and made joshing references to using each other for target practice or blowing each other up.

"Every third Tuesday of the month most of the veterans who live up in the hills around town get together and have lunch," said James, a former submarine sailor who confessed that his return to society has been difficult. "They just talk and eat and make sure everyone's still alive."

Casual visitors to Madrid might not see many of its military veteran residents: They tend to disappear to their homes when the daily crowds of shoppers and tourists arrive.

"The locals I can tolerate," said Ron. "They're mostly nice people. But when tourists go on vacation they tend to leave their brains at home. I don't deal with them too well."

"I don't know why we can't just shoot 'em," James deadpanned. "After all, it's tourist season." The three men nodded grimly at first, then burst out laughing.

Somehow, the mysteries of Madrid felt a little more inscrutable in the presence of these singular men. They waved collegially to the local business owners—primarily the women, that is—as they unlocked their shops for the day.

"Work hard, Darlin!" Ron shouted to a gallery owner pulling out the keys to her front door.

She laughed and engaged with him in a short, friendly chat. Still, the very air around these singular men seemed thick with the sense of preferred isolation. The downtown folks, one and all, nodded respectfully in their direction; they responded with a nod; a half-raised hand with a cigarette pinched between their thumb and forefinger.

When the last of them is gone, one senses, an essential thread in the fabric of Madrid will be pulled forever.

***

Ruth Aber is a former Manhattan podiatrist who quit the city more than twenty years ago to open Mostly Madrid, a consignment art gallery.

Sitting on a rickety bench, gesturing down the dusty street outside her shop, she tells me, "We're an *intentional* community. From the time it was re-settled by Vietnam veterans and artists, the purpose of Madrid has been to create a community where there is no sense of judgment."

Sadly, the days of veterans and starving artists finding a cheap haven in Madrid are fast disappearing. While in 1972 a house on the main street cost a few thousand dollars, in 2024 an 800 square-foot house listed for $239,000. (To be fair, the place did come with a vintage stone dynamite shed.)

When I came through in 2016, Lisa Conley, owner of a pottery studio on the main street, was happy to know I was writing about Madrid—but also understandably concerned about readers who might see the town as some sort of desert paradise.

"*Sixty Minutes* reported on us in the 1980s, and we were bombarded with letters from people who wanted to live here," she recalled. "Several of us had to be a voice of reason and say this is not the kind of place most older people want to come to. There's not a lot of stuff here. A potato at the little store we have can cost you $2.50. My shop building has no insulation in the walls. You have to be really healthy to live here—and a lot of people in their sixties and seventies aren't really healthy."

Which is not to say Madrid is a heartless frontier town that spits out the infirm like spent nutshells. While most of the time the town's disparate communities happily coexist in parallel contentment, when someone needs any kind of help—financial, physical, or emotional—that's when the groups come together as one.

"It doesn't matter who you are or what you believe," says Barbara. "Madroids are all in this together."

For those who need help—struggling artists, displaced veterans, and the odd passing vagabond—Madrid has stitched together a grass roots safety net that involves the entire town. There's a community garden, a weekly food bank at the volunteer fire house and a box where you can drop off used clothes or pick them up.

One Madroid, noodling on his 1960s-vintage left-handed Fender Malibu outside a shop at the south end of town, told me, "It's interesting when you see a friend walk by wearing one of your sweaters."

***

As I sit at my Mine Shaft table, watching Barbara go about seeking likely interview subjects, I notice a sign for Bingo Night. Every month, Madroids of all stripes converge on The Mine Shaft for Bingo—the proceeds to be allocated to one designated local person or family in need. The biggest local charity event of all, though, is the annual He/She Bang, a November drag show gala that raises funds for Madrid's Emergency Medical/Dental Fund. All five performances at the Engine House Theater—adjacent to the Mine Shaft—sell out regularly as audiences pour in from Santa Fe and Albuquerque. (Locals can attend dress rehearsal for five bucks.)

"One thing we make sure of," says Barbara, who's been in charge of the event for the past three years. "The He/She Bang is never political. It's hard, but we make sure to stay away from that."

That was an especially tall order for the most recent He/She Bang, which happened to open five days after the 2024 Presidential election.

"So, we made this year's theme The Apocalypse," she says. "We just decided to go up there and do a show about 'What would happen if we were all just totally fucked?'"

In Madrid, that counts as non-political.

Remarkably, the good people of Madrid—all along the socio/political spectrum—have given a good deal of thought of what they will do if and when American society collapses. In a nutshell, says Barbara, "We're gonna just shut this place down and sit it out together."

Charlie Overbey (Photo by Vanessa Dingwell)

"I've got a generator that would power this whole town!" comes a voice from behind me. It's Charlie Overbey, a musician of some note whose critically acclaimed albums bristle with soulful roots rock. He tours constantly, but calls this patch of the world home.

"I got that generator from a train station in Riverside," he continues, taking the seat next to me. "Just have to fire that sucker up and we're all set."

Born in California, Overbey has made the Madrid area his home for four years after spending a decade based in Santa Fe. Touring takes him everywhere, but he insists he's never been in a place with a more diverse—and happily blended—range of outlooks.

"I was at the Black Bird Saloon, about three miles from here, the other night," he says. "I was sitting with a woman who moved here; a chef from Paris. And with us was an old-school Norteño Hispanic fellow—a total Trumper. Then there was a woman who was considered for Secretary of Education in the Biden Administration. And a rancher. And a cowgirl. And a head designer for Harley-Davidson and his girlfriend, who's been a cover model on *Vogue*. You look around, and you say, 'There's no way on Earth these people should be sitting together!' But they weren't talking about politics; they weren't discussing their diverse opinions. It was just a love fest: they were talking about their families, about taking care of each others' dogs; things like that. Just dealing with each other as people, not as different *kinds* of people."

In some ways, Madrid can be a provocateur's nightmare: It's nigh impossible to offend anyone.

"We had one fellow who moved here from New York," recalls Pam Ellsworth, who runs Dream Gallery. "He wore fishnet shirts, purple skirts, dreadlocks, and mascara. He was all pierced and he drove a purple car. He eventually left, because he couldn't provoke a reaction from us. He was so disappointed!"

***

I take no pride in this, but about an hour into my visit to the Mine Shaft I reflexively pull my iPhone from my pocket and check for emails. Instantly, I am reminded of an essential fact of life in Madrid: There is no cell phone service. In Madrid, if you don't have Wi-Fi—and lots of people here do not—Facebook and X and Instagram are mostly things you hear about from people passing through.

To a city feller, the notion of non-connectivity is somewhat akin to having a pillow held over your face. But when it comes to getting along, that feature may be part of the Madroids' secret sauce.

"We have no choice but to deal with each other eye-to-eye," says Les. "If you've got something to say to someone, you either hide out from them or talk to them about it. And in a town of 300 people, you can't really hide out all that long."

The distancing qualities of the Internet, he says, make it too easy to hold grudges…and fuel them.

"I have an idea that will heal the world," says Les. "Have the microphone on the iPhone double as a breathalyzer, to prevent drunk posting."

Overbey agrees that physical proximity to people you may disagree with is a great damper of resentment. The bad news is, he doesn't think it's really translatable to larger communities.

"When I was living in Oakland, the inner city, there were a lot of people who would say the words, 'I'll support you,' if you were in trouble. But in the end, they don't really show up."

The table grows quiet as Overbey relates a recent story that crystalizes what it can be like when a community really supports someone.

"There was this young woman—everyone here knows her," he says, and those around the table nod.

"She was struggling with some things, and needed to be on medication. Well, her family from back East turned up one day, saying they wanted to take her home because they didn't think she was getting the care she needed."

If there's one thing that sticks in the Madroid's craw, it seems, it's someone telling someone else how to live their life.

"Word got out," Overbey continues, "and all these people came over and stood between the woman and her family. Someone stepped forward and said, 'She gets this medication at this time, and this medication at these times…' and on and on. They knew her whole schedule, and they were making sure she was getting what she needed every day. The Madroids told the family, 'We've got her. She's part of our community. We love her. And fuck you.'"

The family went back East. The young woman stayed with her adopted one.

"We've all been there," says Bill.

"You don't know *where* we've all been," says Barbara.

***

It's getting late at the Mine Shaft. The days of the vets closing the place in the early morning hours are long gone. Before we filter away, though, I venture a question about the town's most hallowed, and most jealously private, spot.

The barely marked dirt roads in and around Madrid lend themselves to lots of scary wrong turns, but if you're lucky one of those turns will turn you up at the Madrid cemetery, on a mesa overlooking town. Madroids are fiercely protective of the place; they won't take outsiders there or even tell them where it is. As you'd expect, the markers are as quirky as the populace: a cast iron derby hat; an oversized gas can; a miniature bicycle. It's the place Madroids expect to end up; a final declaration of their independence—and sometimes of their unexpected compassion.

"Shortly after I came here, this one fellow, kind of a loner, died," recalls Les. "He was a drifter. Nobody really liked the old cuss. He never had anything good to say, and otherwise kept to himself.

"The county was gonna bury him in an unmarked grave, but around town we started talking, and we said, 'Well, we didn't like him, but he was a Madroid.' He deserved to be buried in our cemetery."

It was August, and a team of guys who'd been hanging around the Mine Shaft trudged up the hill with shovels and pickaxes to hack out a grave in the rocky soil. The task took a couple of days. Meanwhile, someone built a coffin. An artist painted a likeness of the fellow on the lid.

As the coffin was lowered into the grave, a circle of Madroids stood around it.

"We buried him up there on the Mesa," says Les. "And I couldn't help but think, 'If Madroids treat someone they don't particularly care for like that, what will they do for people they *do* like?"

The Mine Shaft is closing up. The Madroids and I spill out into the star-strewn night. Some head to their dimly lit homes. Others are off to find somewhere else to have a nightcap or two. In the darkness, someone is singing what might be a jumbled version of "Streets of Laredo."

"That's what I like about Madroids," says Les as we head our separate ways. "We're all here because we're not all *there*."

Paul Anderson & Elvira Diaz

Sparks, Nevada: Trust Matters

It Takes Two Sides to Pull a City Back from the Brink

In lots of American cities, the notion of Paul Anderson and Elvira Diaz sharing lunch at a local Mexican restaurant, laughing and trading good-natured jabs, would be unthinkable.

He's a conservative Republican member of the Sparks, Nevada City Council. She's among the city's most vocal and recognized liberal activists.

"I ran against this guy," she says dryly, gesturing to Anderson, referencing the most recent Sparks City Council election.

Anderson, who's sitting right next to Diaz, smiles and shakes his head.

The flight from New Mexico, a reliably Democratic state, has landed me in northwestern Nevada, an area where liberals and conservatives stand at a population-wide stalemate. The three of us are digging into tacos and quesadillas at *Oh! Mexico*, a little eatery in a Sparks strip mall. Also with us is a mutual friend of Anderson and me: Alison Pratte, a licensed Reno area therapist who, besides working as a marriage counselor, has been recognized by the state of Nevada for her work guiding military and law enforcement people through on-the-job trauma.

Actually, Diaz didn't run for office directly against Anderson: Reno has a runoff system where everyone competes in a primary and the top two vote-getters then oppose each other in the general election. Diaz missed out on the final cut, but just barely: A recount put her out of the running by 42 votes.

The music channel on an overhead TV is rather loudly emitting the classic tones of rancheras music master Vicente Fernández's "Bohemio de Afición," so I need to pay extra attention to Diaz's thickly accented, not to mention florid, storytelling.

"I'm mostly mad at the Democrats," she says regarding her electoral defeat. "I'm a woman, I'm Latina, and I have an accent. They supported the man."

She frowns, shrugs, and returns to her taco.

Diaz first came to the attention of many Reno/Sparks residents in 2013, when the media covered a silent vigil she kept for one hour every Friday outside the federal Courthouse and, later, the office of a Republican representative. Holding a Bible and bowing her head, she held a sign reading, "Justice for Immigrants."

These days she's a tireless proponent of voting rights and election participation—for people of all political parties.

"I don't care if you vote for something that I don't like, or support a candidate I don't," she says. "That's fine. That's democracy."

Elvira pauses a second, then places a hand on Anderson's shoulder. "This guy," she says. "I'll go up to him and say, 'I love you.' And then I'll start screaming, 'But I hate this thing you're supporting!'"

Anderson laughs. Diaz chuckles. Both start nodding as if to say, "So true..."

The unlikely friends were drawn together in the aftermath of George Floyd's 2020 death at the hands of a Minneapolis police officer. That event, combined with community uproar over the 2020 police shooting of an 18-year-old Sparks man who suffered from severe mental illness, led local racial tensions to the breaking point. Next door, in Reno, at least 1,000 people protested downtown—where some participants painted graffiti, burned a U.S. flag, set a small fire outside the city hall, broke in and vandalized the City Council Chambers.

In Sparks, Anderson fretted over whether or not the city's minority community—which is largely Hispanic—might join the fray. Already, City Hall employees had been told not to come to work after someone painted graffiti on its walls. Diaz shared that concern—with the additional fear of how police might react if any demonstrations got out of hand.

***

"We didn't know what was going to happen," Anderson recalls. "Things were really delicate around here."

Clearly, community relations were going downhill fast. That's when the liberal Diaz—a diminutive woman with long streaks of gray hair reaching well beyond her shoulders—approached the conservative Anderson with an idea for a new, open dialogue.

"It was truly Elvira who got it all started in the right direction," says Anderson, whose day job is as an account executive for a logistics firm. He's spent fifty-six of his sixty years in Nevada, nearly all of that in Sparks. When he assumed his council office in the mid-2010s, he thought his biggest challenges would be infrastructure and public safety. But nothing prepared him for the sociological schism that would erupt here and nationwide.

"I saw what was happening in Reno," he says. "We needed to do something. We all needed to talk, I could see that."

In Diaz, he found a kindred spirit: "I didn't want my city to duplicate what happened in Reno," she says. "I wanted us all to have a conversation."

Together, Diaz and Anderson gathered a small group of six or so Latino, Black, and white Sparks residents of various ages, far-right and far-left, plus another city council member, for a series of candid conversation sessions.

The cast was assembled, but the early going was rough: The participants seemed fixated on expressing their grievances, or the ways they felt they'd been misunderstood. No one seemed able to stake out common ground, much less an elevated sense of each other's humanity.

That's were my friend Alison, the therapist and counselor, came in: She suggested the group draw inspiration from one of the most celebrated mediation efforts in modern history.

"I asked Paul if he knew anything about Nelson Mandela's Truth and Reconciliation program in South Africa," she says. "It involved having the different groups, who used to be in opposition to each other, talk frankly about everything that happened between them. And in the end, the aim was to pursue forgiveness, rather than prosecution."

The idea resonated with the group.

"So, now we had a reconciliation movement in Sparks," says Diaz. "We realized that it's not enough just to try and stop fighting and breaking windows and calling each other names. We needed to understand why people act this way."

For several sessions, the core group simply got to know each other;

focusing not on the issues that divided them but on the goals they shared for their community.

Not everyone Anderson knew in city government was pleased with the idea.

"At first, there was some real resistance," he recalls. "People asked me, 'Why are you even having this conversation with those people? They're on the other side!'"

But Anderson wasn't discouraged. Before long, as participants followed a more conciliatory model, he said, "We were having real conversations with each other."

Anderson even convinced Sparks' City Manager to buy into the effort.

"So now we had the City of Sparks officially sponsoring the event," he says. "That really got our forum program off the ground."

Once the core participants were comfortable with each other, the conversation was opened to the entire community. For the first open forum, only about twenty residents joined in. But word spread that something constructive was happening during those sessions, which were held on the meeting app Zoom. About twice as many community members logged in for the second meeting.

At that point, the group had very little in the shape of a formal agenda.

"We just gave everybody in the community space to talk about what was on their minds," says Diaz.

Anderson and Diaz were dismayed at first, when simmering frustrations began to boil over.

"There were some angry people," Anderson recalls, then he catches himself. "No, in fact, I would venture to say most of it was angry people. Yeah. *Very* angry people."

From anger, he says, the general mood moved to "uncomfortable."

"The important thing was to give people a space where they could voice their frustrations," he says. "Our police chief came in, and he spoke a little bit about his concerns—but most importantly he came to listen."

It was then that Anderson and Diaz began employing in earnest the lessons of Nelson Mandela: pursuing a model where all sides, no matter how they had behaved toward each other in the past, could make a future together.

"We needed to start seeing the value of each other," says Diaz. "You can use your energy to escalate conflict, or you can use it to get together and make a real community."

The group met regularly for about a year, welcoming new waves of interested members of the community as they progressed. In response to their work, in 2021 the city created a formal Equity and Inclusion Advisory Board—with a member from each of the city's five wards plus two members appointed by the mayor—charged specifically with keeping channels open between Sparks' various population groups and the city government. (No surprise, Diaz was named its original chair.)

As you might expect, any committee with the name Equity and Inclusion faces a certain kind of peril in Donald Trump's America. The harsh reality is, any conservative participating in one would most likely be courting political crossfire. The group's February 2025 meeting was cancelled. No one is talking about re-convening.

***

Still, that brief flourish of open conversation has made an indelible difference for the people of Sparks.

Most importantly, the group's recommendations resulted in nothing less than a revolution in the way law enforcement polices the city's streets. Thanks to new approaches to neighborhood policing, officers and the people they've sworn to protect are increasingly seeing each other not as rivals, but as partners.

"Police are actually spending informal time in the schools, and in neighborhoods where in the past they might have only gone to respond to a crime," says Anderson.

You'll find cops taking time off from their beats to play basketball with local kids. Officers will stop at children's lemonade stands to buy a drink. Or they'll drop in on a business just to say hello.

"I got to ride with the Sparks police a month ago," says Anderson, his eyes widening. "A lot of folks knew the officers by their first names. And our officers knew them."

Diaz fondly recalls encountering a Sparks police officer at a community event, sponsored by the local Catholic Church, aimed at helping undocumented local people understand their legal rights. He introduced himself to the group in Spanish.

"Not very *good* Spanish," she allows with a smile, "but he tried."

Responding to community reluctance to report a crime for fear of immigration hassles, Diaz says, the officer responded, "Don't be afraid to report it. We won't do anything to you." (This was, of course, before the 2025 nationwide ICE crackdown, but the sentiment was clear: *We are your police department, too.*)

The meeting, in a large Catholic church, was attended by 2,400 people plus dignitaries including a state senator and the Nevada secretary of state.

"The priest who organized the event asked me, 'Who was your favorite person here?'" Diaz recalls. "I said, 'The policeman from Sparks!'"

Most importantly, Anderson says, the group (and its outreach) has forced once-totally isolated segments of Sparks' population to look each other in the eye and acknowledge, if not complete agreement on issues, at least complete agreement on each other's worth.

"For me, personally, the biggest thing was in everyone seeing that they had more similarities than you would otherwise think," he says. "The social isolation is understandable: We tend to hang with people that are like us; people who we can feel comfortable without even thinking about it.

"I mean, look at me and Elvira. We don't live far apart at all; our neighborhoods are just basically across a roadway from each other. But before this I would never have headed over to her side on my own, and she would never have come over to mine."

Diaz nods and glances up at Anderson's face.

"But I would caution people about one thing," he continues. "If you sincerely say, 'I want to learn from people that are different from me, you've got to be willing to get a little uncomfortable. And, honestly, when we first started this, it was uncomfortable."

Diaz glances at me and nods with a *you can say that again* look.

"There's no way everybody's going to be the same," she says, leaning closer to me. "And everybody has to learn that that's okay."

Lunch time is over. The four of us head out to the parking lot and begin to head in four directions. But I have one last question.

"You know, there's going to be another George Floyd disaster someday, and maybe someday soon," I venture. "How do you think you'll respond?"

Anderson pauses.

"I'd like to think we'll be more proactive next time," he says. "And I'm counting on the things we've done already to put us in a better place to begin with."

"And maybe we'll get our group back together!" Diaz adds.

Anderson smiles at the thought.

"Honestly," he says, "I think one of the best things I've ever done was to not be afraid; to have these important conversations with people who are different than me. No matter how uncomfortable it was."

Anderson and Diaz head for their cars. Alison and I say so-long as she heads off for a therapy session with clients.

"You know," she sighs, "sometimes I think all the United States needs is a good marriage counselor."

Man Night

Orange County, California: The Fires of Friendship

On Man Night, All Voices Are Heard

There's no drive in the country I love more than the one from the area of Lake Tahoe to Southern California, rolling along the eastern slopes of the Sierra Nevada, catching sight of Mount Whitney's silver snowcap to my right and the parched environs of Death Valley to my left. Even the home stretch, coursing down Interstate 5 through the Angeles National Forest, knowing any minute I'll be plunging into the nation's sprawling-est metropolis, the defiant diversity of America's West Coast spreads across my windshield like a Cinemascope movie.

I arrive in Newport Beach shortly after dusk, just in time to take my seat around a backyard fire where six old friends have graciously invited me to join them.

It's one of those southern California winter nights when the air is damp enough to see your breath, even with the temperature hovering near fifty.

The friends—middle-age professional guys, some of whom have known each other for decades—are slumped low in Adirondack chairs, their legs stretching toward a metal wash bin doubling as a fire pit. Above their heads spread the gnarly branches of a Chinese elm, the limbs decked with lights that sway in a soft breeze, glowing yellow against the darkening sky.

A marine level inversion has kept this neighborhood on a bluff above Newport's back bay, shrouded in fog all day. But now a sharply divided half-moon is casting pale light on the proceedings.

The guys call these regular gatherings Man Night.

As you might expect, the friends spend some time sharing catch-up info regarding kids and spouses, work and church. But most amazingly, in a time when the practice is often considered social suicide, the men are talking politics.

***

And I don't mean that all-on-the-same-page, "Aren't those other guys awful?" kind of political chitchat. These fellows, all in their late forties or early fifties, cover the political spectrum: From Newsmax to Fox to CNN to MSNBC (now, MS NOW) and beyond. And they don't pull their punches.

There's James, a California land acquisition and management executive and a self-described "center right" voter. Miles, CFO of an Orange County real estate development company, considers himself a centrist. Joe, partner in an Orange County law firm's litigation group, is a dyed-in-the-wool conservative. Brian, managing director of an Irvine Debt and Structured Finance team, is, if anything, even farther right than Joe. Ryan, owner of a chain of oil change businesses, sits right of center and is seen by the group as something of a moderator. And sitting on my right is my son Ben, marketing executive for a medical device manufacturer and an unapologetic liberal.

Significantly, Brian and Ben—the two men here who sit at the farthest extremes of the political spectrum—have been friends since childhood. I first met Brian when he was barely fifteen years old, during one of the regular Tuesday Night Dinners my late wife, Cindy, and I hosted for years at our home in Washington, DC's Georgetown.

Those dinners, freewheeling affairs that drew kids from all over DC and nearby Virginia and Maryland, were the closest thing most of them would ever get to experiencing that great European tradition of a salon. All points of view were welcome; the topics changed too swiftly for recrimination. *The Washington Post* thought enough about those weekly gatherings—which spanned the better part of a decade—to run a story about them.

I like to think those Tuesday Night Dinners had a lot to do with the diversity of viewpoints—and non-judgy attitudes—that prevail among my children. Ben, Tiffany, Nicholas and Zachary, now spread geographically across the country, run the gamut from pretty liberal to mighty conservative. (My stepdaughter, Erica, would rather have a tooth pulled than discuss politics at all.) And here's the thing: My kids love each other to bits and, to my mind, enjoy nothing better than just hanging out and shooting the breeze.

I've heard it said that a mix like that, of kids who clearly think for themselves, is indicative of superior parenting.

I may have heard it said by me, but whatever.

When Ben's wife, Bronwen, heard I was working on this book, she insisted that my itinerary include a stop in California for Man Night. "Ben's friends are all over the place," she said. "But they'd donate a lung to each other if they needed it." She was, of course, correct.

So, as we sit around the fire pit, liberal Ben takes no umbrage when conservative James observes, "If I met Ben at a dinner party and he was, you know, espousing his belief in the benefits of an inefficient government, I'd be like, 'This guy is a dipshit.'"

Ben tilts his head and smiles. It kind of feels like he's heard the dipshit thing before.

"But I know Ben as a friend, and I know he's not a dipshit. And even if he were a dipshit, I wouldn't care, because he's my friend. I love him."

At the moment we are gathered here, in December 2024, America is in the always-interesting transition period between two Presidential administrations: President-elect Donald Trump is in the process of nominating his Cabinet, and the guys around the firepit are variously elated, cautious, horrified and unimpressed.

Brian gets a polite chuckle from Ben when he declares that "liberals got their ass kicked" in the last election.

"Really?" Ben says. "It seems to me the needle shifted a little to the right, but that's about all."

"I think we're in for a dangerous time," says Ryan. "I hope I'm wrong, but Trump is being reckless with the people he's putting into place. There seems to be no regard for the long-term consequences."

"He's gonna do it right," Brian insists. "He going to try to keep everybody happy and not divide the country more."

"I'm kind of worried about having a Vivek-Musk Administration," says Ben, alluding to the two billionaires Trump recently assigned the task of streamlining government. (This was before Elon Musk's Department of Government Efficiency (DOGE) flared comet-like across the continent, and

as I write these words I am reminded of the absolute futility of trying to tie any chapter of any book to a particular political moment.)

"To me," says Joe, "that is the most exciting thing I've ever heard. I know we disagree on that."

"I'm just not excited about it," Ben says.

"I get it," Joe continues. "I've heard you say before that certain things should be left to the government, and I'm okay if those things are not left to the government."

"Well," Ben responds, "there are going to be millions of federal government workers who don't have jobs. Will everything keep going fine? Maybe. It just might. We'll see."

"I don't think a lot of those workers do much work," Joe suggests.

"Oh, there's no doubt about that!" Ben says. "We have friends! We call them Beltway Bandits!"

"Yep!" Brian chimes in. "Ben and I grew up in DC…"

"People who built a career…" says Ben.

"…doing nothing!" Brian enthuses.

I marvel at how the two old friends, political polar opposites, manage to finish each other's sentences, excitedly jumping on a point where they find common ground.

Joe seizes on that notion, adding that he believes friends are willing to give friends a benefit of the doubt that might have to be earned (or discounted) elsewhere.

For one thing, he says, this group had developed much love and respect for each other before they knew each other's political tendencies. Random strangers thrust into similar conversational alleys might not fare as well.

"The fact is," Joe says, "I'd say friendship does grease the wheels when it comes to political disagreements."

Does preserving a friendship, I ask, sometimes involve just biting your tongue?

I receive a quick, and unanimous, "No!"

"That's just kind of sad, isn't it?" asks James. "How can you maintain a friendship, or any kind of relationship, for that matter, and say, 'I can't share what I think?'" What you think, he insists, is part of who you are, whether someone disagrees with you or not. "If you're hiding your thoughts or your feelings or your beliefs, then that's not much different from just being disconnected from the people who disagree with you."

Joe chimes in with what I find to be a remarkable desire: To revive what he sees as the spirit of discourse that once defined America—before he was even born—but has since been smothered.

"What we're doing around this fire," he says, "is what people did traditionally fifty, sixty, or seventy years ago. It was actually normal—believe it or not—for people to talk about politics, and to respect each other enough to say, 'Okay, we disagree and that's not a bad thing.'"

I feel compelled to mention the case of two dear friends of my parents, fellow parishioners at St. Mary's Catholic Church in Dumont, NJ, who could not abide our family's support of Lyndon B. Johnson versus Barry Goldwater in 1964. Their friendship was shattered over the matter—putting me in a particularly uncomfortable position, as the woman was one of my teachers at the church parochial school.

"I know what this is about," my mother said when she saw a less-than-perfect grade on my report card. "Do you want me to talk to her?"

I do not believe I have ever begged harder in the negative for anything in my life.

So, the division of friends by politics is nothing new. But why does it now seem more the norm than an isolated phenomenon? The Man Night gang agrees this has a lot to do with technology, and the way it is becoming a poor substitute for interpersonal contact.

Around the firepit, a general consensus grows that friendships can be an antidote to the steady stream of demonization fed to Americans by media companies that thrive on division.

"I mean, just look at your friends, your *real* friends," says Joe. "Do those social media algorithms describe who they are? They've created this *us-versus-them* story about everything. And I just don't buy it."

We have emptied a bottle of bourbon, and Miles has corked it and placed it in the fire. Immediately, Joe realizes the horizontally oriented bottle is pointed directly at him.

"Seriously, man," Joe barks, "could you please point that bottle upwards? You've got that cork aimed right at my eye."

"That's a terrible thing to do to a man just because you don't like his politics," says James.

With a piece of wood, Miles shifts the bottle so its neck points upward. And within moments, the heated air inside the bottle sends the cork flying. It falls harmlessly within a foot or two of the fire pit. The bottle begins to sink into the coals.

"Coulda blinded me for life," Joe mutters.

The discussion returns to the tragic nationwide phenomenon of families and friends being torn apart by political and social issues. A 2023 study by the American Psychiatric Association found that one in five Americans had become estranged from a family member, blocked a family member on social media, or skipped a family event due to disagreements on controversial topics. And one-third had engaged in a heated political discussion with a family member.

What, I ask, do these six guys have going for them that those people don't?

Ben points immediately to the element that seems to underlie most of the conditions cited by the study: It would appear few of those estranged family members are seeing each other face-to-face.

"A really important dynamic of this group is that we see each other," he says. "When you're online, it's easy to build paper dragons and just go to war."

"We are actual friends here, in the old-fashioned sense," adds James. "I don't even go on Facebook. I don't know how to follow anyone. So I'm not getting bombarded with comments and emails.

"I mean, if Brian over there was just smothering me online with post after post of his usual whackadoodle comments, I'd be like, 'Get this guy out of here.' I'd just unfollow him.

"Here's an example: I guess I would agree with Brian on more policy matters than I agree with Ben. Still, sitting over a fire with Ben, I can engage and respect him as a person. But if Brian, who I agree with more, started messaging and commenting and emailing me every day, I'd cut him off. That's the difference between a real relationship and, say, a Facebook one."

Brian offers a case in point: "Ben and I are also on text groups, and we'll get kind of heated."

Ben smiles. "We bash each other," he says.

"Right!" Brian continues. "*Bash* each other! But then we get together in person, and we can just talk. We have a civilized conversation. It's not where you're posting and just using your thumbs and you somehow feel more free to be offensive."

Although Brian is one of Ben's oldest friends, he's the newest participant in Man Night, having moved to Newport Beach only recently. As such, the group has playfully dangled full Man Night membership just out of reach.

"Talk about being offended," he adds. "I've been pledging to this group for four years now. I've still gotta drive and buy beer. I belong to one of the most prestigious organizations in Newport Beach but I can't get into this group."

"Be patient," James deadpans. "The membership committee only meets on the fourth Sunday of Leap Year."

There's laughter, but then a silence creeps around the firepit. To these friends, the mere idea of being offensive to each other is, it seems, an untenable proposition.

"I guess what I'm trying to say," Brian says, "is that this country has lost the art of disagreement."

Another silence.

"Well," James ventures, "we've never really offended each other, have we? I mean, have we ever, in all our time together, ever had an instance of anybody being greatly offended?"

"Yes," Miles shoots back, and James looks genuinely surprised.

"Really?" he asks.

"Yeah," Miles continues. "Remember that time when someone sent out a text message and accidentally included a neighbor's wife?"

There's a collective inhalation among the men. It's clear no further elaboration is desired.

"Yes, there was that," James murmurs.

Almost imperceptibly, the heads around the circle turn to Ryan, who has emerged as the group's voice of reason. The guys jokingly call him "Pastor," partially because he actually once took a weekend seminary course, but also because he has a knack for tying together disparate threads of thought.

"I think it's all about knowing people," he says. "And to know people, you have to see people. When you navigate life together—marriage, parenthood, neighboring—you can tell yourself, 'Oh, yeah, okay. Maybe this guy's got a sideways mind, but he's actually a good person.'"

He gestures toward Ben.

"I mean, take Ben," he says. "He lives in Newport Beach, one of the most conservative places in Orange County, which is itself conservative. When someone here meets a crazy liberal like Ben, they might first want to avoid him. But soon they see he actually cares about his friends and his family, and that he's also a high-quality human being."

Ben nods in acknowledgement.

"I mean, *generally* speaking a high-quality human being," Ryan hastens to add.

"But when people here in Newport Beach meet someone like Ben, who thinks differently than they do, and they see what a quality person he is, well, that helps take away any stereotypes they might have about *other* people like Ben. And by that I mean crazy liberals."

"You can extend that beyond politics," Ben adds. "Empathy builds empathy. You hear a lot about how rich Christians don't love the poor. But the real problem is, they don't know the poor."

The circle nods in agreement.

After an hour or so, the subject of politics is clearly exhausted ("We usually only talk politics about twenty percent of the time, if that," Ben says). The guys seem relieved to retreat to the usual exchanges concerning sports, and family, and Grace Fellowship Church, the congregation they are all a part of. Joe has brought some mighty fine cigars to go with the second bottle of bourbon.

As I gaze into the firepit, rolling cigar smoke over my tongue and letting the friends' conversations morph into a pleasing hum, I think about a fracture within my own family, with a guy I've known since I was fifteen. Somewhere along the way he ventured far down one political path while I remained in my moderate perch—at least I think I did. Certainly, I did not from his perspective as he began to view me as a radical danger to the American Way of Life. Our widening split played out on the pages of Facebook, first in dismissive insults in response to political posts of mine, later in a series of angry memes.

We were separated by a thousand miles. The one and only time we've spoken in the past six years, at his mother's funeral, we looked at each other, smiled and hugged. The last words we said to each other were, "I love you."

I still love that guy, and I suspect he loves me, too. But just after the last election, he posted on my Facebook page the assertion that no one who voted for my Presidential candidate could ever be a Christian. He meant me. And for some reason, that was a bridge too far.

"You are a good man," I wrote to him. But his words were too hurtful to endure. I blocked someone I've known for more than fifty years. Though we were no longer close, I still feel an empty spot in my heart. I hold onto that one tender moment we shared at a funeral, and I know that, were we face-to-face, sharing dinners and family weekends as we did long ago, we would be friendly to this day. Or at least I hope we would.

Little domestic dramas like that have played out, often in ways far more dramatic, among hundreds of millions of American family members. I wonder if it's easier for friends, who choose each other and so are more invested in sustaining those relationships, no matter what their political stances are.

"So, what do you think?" I hear Ben ask the group. "Is, maybe, this tribe more important to us than our political tribe?"

"I'll tell you one thing," says James, "I will always choose this tribe over who I vote for."

Seguaro in the proposed Arizona I-11 Corridor

Sonoran Desert, Arizona: Alliances in the Wilderness

The Road to Unity Can Have Four Lanes and a Median

If you've never heard a saguaro cactus sing, then you have most likely never stood amidst a remote Sonoran Desert cluster of them while a gentle wind coursed through their spiny bristles, sighing soft verses of dreamlike desolation.

It is Spring. The desert—which I've barely left even on the long drive from Southern California to this spot—is still awaiting the hotbox of summer, and so even in the late morning, the desert scrub rustles with passing denizens. A loping jackrabbit. A scuttling Gambel's quail. And high atop the saguaro, twenty feet up, burst the white-and-yellow blossoms that draw bats and bees for their annual duties as prolific pollinators.

From North Sandario Road, about a mile to the west, the throaty *blatt* of a diesel truck engine rumbles across the landscape. The aural intrusion fades into the distance, then it's gone.

If federal highway planners have their way, that momentary intrusion will become a twenty-four-hour roar at the spot where I am standing. In legislative offices far from this peaceful idyl, drawing boards trace the path of the anticipated Interstate Highway 11. Promising to alleviate traffic tie-ups that have plagued nearby Tucson for decades, I-11 would shuttle traffic in a loop to the city's west, through this delicate desert countryside and north toward Phoenix. It's all part of a grand design that would create a commercial lifeline from Mexico to Canada.

For an environmentalist—both conservative and liberal—that's not a good enough reason to carve a 1,000-foot-wide corridor of asphalt and concrete through one of the continent's most delicate habitats.

I've been directed here by Carolyn Campbell, a longtime executive director of the Coalition for Sonoran Desert Protection. Experiencing the place, she clearly believes, is the only way to understand its quiet power.

At Campbell's suggestion, we'd met at Raging Sage, a boutique coffee shop in Tucson, where we sat together in a shady courtyard.

"The corridor they're proposing," she said, "comes within 1,500 feet of Sonora National Park." Her exasperation was palpable. "It's 300 feet from Ironwood State Forest. And that would be after it's built—not considering all the space needed for construction."

As we chatted, I couldn't help but notice Campbell was staring at a spot above my head and behind me.

"Look at that!" she finally said, wrapping her slender fingers around her cup of tea. "There's a dove's nest right above you!"

I turned in my chair and, in the dense leaves of an overhanging orange tree, I barely made out the silhouette of two birds, cooing in their comfy home of twigs. I would never have noticed them, but Carolyn—crowned "Queen of the Environmentalists" at her 2024 retirement bash—has an eye for things like that.

Carolyn's soft smile faded as she returned to the subject at hand. So sensitive is the proposed route, she said, that the U.S. Bureau of Reclamation routinely turns down applications for cell towers within its boundaries.

"And now they want to put a freeway in there?" she gasped. "A freeway? That was the 1960s solution to everything." She shook her head.

A proud and outspoken liberal, Campbell nevertheless credits conservative Republicans with many of Arizona's most historically significant environmental advances. She offered a nod to the late Arizona Senator Jim Kolbe, who was instrumental in securing millions of dollars in federal earmarks to set aside Sonoran Desert land. He was the primary force behind elevating Saguaro National Monument to National Park status. In all likelihood, Arizona's 4,800-acre Canoa Ranch Conservation Park and 45,000-acre Las Cienegas National Conservation Area would never have been established without his backing.

Of course, she hastened to add, Kolbe's heyday came in a very different political climate—one in which a staunchly conservative Arizona

Republican like John McCain could co-sponsor the 2003 Climate Stewardship Act, the first major bipartisan bill to limit greenhouse gasses. And before that, Arizona Senator Barry Goldwater—Mr. Conservative himself—provided the heft to push the Arizona Wilderness Act of 1984 across the finish line.

"I know for a fact there are still people on both sides of the political divide who are passionate about the environment," Campbell said, leaning over her tea. Then she sat back with a sigh. "But these days no one talks about their politics. Frankly, I don't know how many people I work with are conservatives, and I don't ask. But trust me; they are there." Now, she said, politics just gets in the way of accomplishing things. "I don't want to talk about political parties."

Neither do I, I assured her. I'm just trying to find those sweet spots—in this case, environmental ones—that are no-brainers for people no matter what their party.

The northern reaches of the proposed I-11 corridor plow through staunchly Republican territory, most of it farmland. To the more populated south—closer to Tucson proper—the voting population becomes decidedly more mixed. Whatever their political affiliation, though, Carolyn believes those elbow room-loving folks are of one mind when it comes to their natural habitat.

"Those people all moved out there to find peace of mind," she said. "A peaceful landscape. Now they're looking at their homes being taken out. When you get out there, you'll see."

***

That challenge has brought me to the shadows of these towering, singing cactuses. Along the desolate shoulders of North Sandario Road—where that bellowing big rig interrupted my idyll—stand tight clusters of mailboxes, sometimes as many as three dozen in one grouping. Each box represents a homestead; another person who traded sidewalks and sewage service for a little slice of Sonoran seclusion.

The folks in Washington, DC, would do well to chat with the people they represent around here. It's one thing to sit in a Freedom Caucus meeting at the Capitol and rail against environmental concerns at the expense of commerce. It's quite another to be a social conservative, passionate about the natural environment around you, and discover your beloved wilderness sits in the bullseye of so-called progress.

The reality has been sinking in here for as long as I-11 has been on the drawing board. Just a few hundred yards from the site of my Saguaro cactus epiphany, a rural community called Avra Foothill Estates stands to be obliterated by the current route of I-11. The owner of a day camp in the community told me he has no illusions regarding the project: "It would take away our livelihood if it did happen."

I find nothing but agreement as I drive north toward the solidly conservative farming town of Red Rock. When I venture into the cozy darkness of the Red Rock Bar—a deceptively plain double-wide trailer that offers friendly service and a surprisingly varied Southwestern menu—I soon learn the more liberal opponents of I-11 down south have some enthusiastic allies in this conservative bastion.

"I don't want to be in any book," cautions a bearded middle-aged guy, echoing a phrase I'm hearing whenever I talk with conservatives, no matter where I encounter them. "But you can tell 'em that highway'll just cut any number of farms in half. Now, how is a guy supposed to get his equipment across four lanes of interstate?"

He shakes his head.

"Morons."

Even organizations traditionally from the Right and Left are blending in a chorus of protest: In August 2021 Arizona Sportsmen for Wildlife Conservation submitted a letter urging that the I-11 corridor be shifted east from the wilderness and into direct alignment with the existing Interstate that passes through Tucson. The thirty signees represented a wide political spectrum ranging from the conservative Christian Hunters of America to the left-leaning Theodore Roosevelt Conservation Partnership.

***

Along the route back to Tucson along North Sandario Road, my car's tires emit a distinct *clunk-clunk* as I pass over a small concrete bridge. Beneath it flows a dark ribbon of water: a monument to bipartisan Arizonan environmentalism.

The Central Arizona Project—an eighty-foot-wide, 300-mile course from here to the Colorado River—is the lifeblood of southern Arizona. Without the cooperation of Republicans and Democrats, it probably wouldn't be here—and, significantly, neither would the environmentally friendly features protecting the desert and animals that line its banks.

The notion of an aqueduct to south central Arizona was first advanced in the U.S. Congress in 1946 by Senator Carl Hagan, a Democrat who represented Arizona in Congress even before Arizona became a state. The

Methuselah of Congress, Hagan arrived in Washington, DC when William Howard Taft was President and left when Richard Nixon was in the White House.

Hagan lived to age ninety-four, but not long enough to shepherd the aqueduct to completion. That job fell into the capable—and famously conservative—hands of his successor, Barry Goldwater, making the Central Arizona Project one of Arizona's most impactful bipartisan infrastructure efforts.

From the Panama Canal to Hoover Dam to the Interstate Highway System, you'd be hard-pressed to find big federal projects prior to the 1960s that took into serious consideration their impacts on local wildlife. But Arizonans—no matter what their political stripe—have always been tightly tethered to their environment. When the notion of a cross-desert canal was hatched by Democrats and promoted by Republicans, the same question was raised by city folk, environmentalists and ranchers alike: *What about the animals*?

***

Finding a likely dirt road heading toward the canal, I drive to the end, where a long, raised hill stretches from one end of my field of view to the other and beyond: the canal's western berm. A barbed wire-topped chain link fence tops the berm, and fifty feet or so before that my closer approach is blocked by another wire fence posted: "United States Government Property/NO Trespassing/Se Prohibe Entrar/Violators Will Be Prosecuted."

And just in case the would-be trespasser can read neither English nor Spanish, there's also a symbol of a human figure with a red line through it.

I walk parallel to the fence, looking out for rattlesnakes and dodging the spines of a low-lying prickly pear cactus—in full bloom with yellow blossoms—until I come to a wide break in the berm, an open area beneath which, clearly, a tunnel has been excavated for the canal.

The first fence ends at the opening, but I know enough to proceed no further. This is one of scores of wildlife bridges across the canal, a scrub-strewn monument to Arizona's history of bipartisan environmentalism.

After the original aqueduct plans were released, a coalition of conservative and liberal environmentalists—along with concerned ranchers—helped determine where animal crossings should be built. (For a 1982 University of Arizona study, before the ditch was dug, researchers fitted bighorn sheep with walkie talkie-sized transmitters, then sat back to see where they preferred to traverse the landscape.)

My point here is, for the better part of a century, Arizona liberals and conservatives have been pretty much on the same page when it comes to balancing human use of the environment with preservation of natural resources. What's more, no matter who I've spoken to in the state—Right, Left, and Center—that shared longing for balance remains.

The difference seems to be: whereas in decades past liberals and conservatives proudly marched arm-in-arm on environmental issues, these days, there's little perceived upside to acknowledging each other's shared values.

Meanwhile, the water takes its course; the cactus sings its song. And, for now at least, the traffic remains at bay.

Casa Church

Tucson, Arizona: Welcome the Stranger

Threading a Political Needle,
Some Evangelicals Still Minister to Immigrants

The southern Arizona light pouring into Jennifer Tompkins' office is bright and beaming with promise. Out in the hallway, there's laughter and a little bit of running as the staff at Casas Church, an Evangelical mega congregation, prepares for the coming rush of summer programs.

I'm sticking around Tucson to talk with Tompkins, the church's outreach pastor, about her former work as Executive Director of Tucson Refugee Ministry. The topic is immigration, and as tactfully as I can, I ask why, when it comes to this particular subject, Evangelicals have earned a reputation as people who, well, how shall I put this…

"Don't care about anybody?" she interjects, mercifully.

Well, I stammer, since you put it that way…

You don't have to be a Bible scholar to be familiar with Christian Scripture's abundance of sympathetic sentiment toward immigrants. "The foreigner residing among you must be treated as your native-born," the Book of Leviticus commands the Jewish people.

"I was a stranger and you invited me in," Jesus declares in the Gospel of Matthew.

"You shall love the stranger," cautions the Book of Deuteronomy, "for you were strangers in the land of Egypt."

Plus, every Sunday School child knows that Jesus and his family are the Bible's most celebrated undocumented aliens, having snuck into Egypt to avoid the wrath of King Herod.

Still, here is Evangelical icon Franklin Graham—whose charity, Samaritan's Purse, has fed and clothed millions of needy people around the world—defending radical immigrant deportation to the conservative news outlet Newsmax: "That has nothing to do with compassion. It has to do with what's right to do."

And listen to Evangelical Pastor Paul Rigney telling Religion News Service, on the subject of immigration, that while the Bible does on occasion command pity and compassion, "It also says in various places that there are times when pity and compassion are entirely inappropriate."

Maybe the Evangelical church's reputation as being hard-core anti-immigrant is due to the fact that in the Evangelical church—like everywhere else—the biggest mouths get the biggest microphones. I say this, by the way, as one who has been affiliated with Evangelical churches for three-quarters of my life.

I've decided to stick with Arizona for this particular subject for two reasons: a) Few places have felt the impact of immigration—both legal and not—more than this border state, and b) Since Arizona ranks near the middle of the pack when it comes to religiosity of its residents, it seems like a likely place for a healthy debate on the subject of how Christians should address, for example, the Apostle Peter's exhortation to "Show hospitality to one another without grumbling."

And wouldn't you know it, I've found a core of immigrant-friendly Evangelicals in, of all places, Southern Arizona, as sizzling an immigration hotspot as you will find.

***

The good people of Casas Church are as socially conservative as they come: Their opposition to abortion is steadfast. Gay marriage is not a thing. The notion of transgender students competing in sports with opposite members of their birth sex is unthinkable.

And if you ask them, their take on caring for immigrants—especially refugees—is likewise rooted in their literal reading of Scripture.

"There's no nationalism in the Bible," says Casas Church's Tompkins. "In the Bible, it's very clear that God is calling on the Jewish people to gather all the nations to go with them—especially when Abraham's leaving for the Promised Land. He's out there gathering people, saying 'Come with us! Love your neighbor as yourself. Bring the people along.'

"They're sure not saying 'Secure the borders. Don't let anybody in.' That never happened in the Bible."

Tompkins became Executive Director of Tucson Refugee Ministry in 2019, inheriting the position from its late founder, Cherie Gray, who'd started the foundation in 2003 to serve refugee populations in and around the city. Besides immigrants pouring across the U.S./Mexico border, sixty-eight miles to the south, Tucson has some 15,000 registered refugees: large populations of Afghan, Congolese, Syrian, Vietnamese, Ukrainian and Sudanese asylum seekers—all of whom find themselves hurled head-first into a society that is, in nearly every way, foreign to them.

Tompkins clarifies that she is well aware of the important distinction to be made between refugees—people here at the invitation of the U.S. government as they try to escape persecution in their home countries—and undocumented immigrants, the millions who have, over the past several years, poured across the U.S. Southern border in violation of federal law.

Still, she says, "We never ask about someone's legal status. We're just here to help people."

Under Gray, TRM's main focus was a simple one: to build relationships between newcomers and Tucsonians. Upon assuming leadership of the group, Kansas-born Tompkins, drawing on what she calls her "Practical Midwest Side," decided to launch a more substantive program, dealing with the practical needs of refugees and immigrants.

"Early on, we had a group of young boys from Africa that became obsessed with finding members of their tribe—because they came here from a tribal culture," she says. "Sadly, they ended up in a gang and died. It occurred to me: Why can't we help those young people find each other in a healthy, safe place?"

TRM is doing that now, inviting young refugees and immigrants to connect with each other through organized activities and community centers.

Engaging with the refugee community, Tompkins and TRM's volunteers discovered that many of those newcomers—who'd been forced to leave high-level careers and professions behind as they escaped their home countries—were now languishing in menial jobs.

"We had an Afghan neurosurgeon who was working here as a dishwasher," she says. "An airport manager was cleaning houses. So we started Arrive and Thrive, a program to help re-establish people in their old professions."

In many cases, TRM volunteers dive head-first into the immigration bureaucracy, contacting newcomers' former countries to track down their college transcripts and professional credentials—clearing the way for them to enter U.S. colleges and universities or, in some cases, pick up their careers where they left off.

How I wish, sitting here listening to Tompkins enumerate the forward-thinking work of TRM, that this was the predominant narrative in the Evangelical Church. So, why isn't it?

The problem isn't the story. The problem is: Who's telling it?

I've been in the media long enough to understand why the spectacle of Evangelicals opposing charitable programs to aid immigrants is an irresistible angle: Perceived hypocrisy is catnip for news outlets. Also, conflicts within faith groups are a favorite topic for reporters and editors who may not have a grasp on the nuances of belief, but have a firm hold on the notion of supposed brethren in Christ going at each other.

Worse, the Evangelical community seems all too happy to feed that appetite for conflict with any number of public skirmishes. On one side is Southern Baptist Theological Seminary's Walter Strickland, who wrote "standing on the side of Dreamers (children of undocumented aliens) is the job of Christians." Tearing into such positions, Evangelical writer Jon Harris told *The Federalist*, "Many Southern Baptists believe the gospel hinges on Jesus' redemptive work, not leftist politics."

Evangelical suspicion of immigrants is nothing new: A 2013 study by *Politics and Religion Journal* in Houston, Texas, found that fifty-five percent of Evangelicals believed immigrants are a burden because they take away jobs, and fifty-eight percent said they threaten traditional American customs and values. Going even further back, in the mid-1880s Protestant fears about waves of European immigration caused church members to affiliate with the anti-immigrant Know-Nothing Party.

The pendulum seemed to swing the other way following World War II, when the major Christian denominations championing migrant resettlement were as conservative as they come, including Southern Baptists, the Assemblies of God, and the Mennonites. Then came the rise of the Evangelical Right in the 1980s and beyond—nurtured and openly supported by political conservatives—which promoted hawkish views on immigrants: Jerry Falwell, Jr., Franklin Graham, Ralph Reed and James Dobson were members of President Donald Trump's 2016 "Board of Evangelical Advisors" which, insisting they were embracing Biblical principles, loudly supported border walls and tougher border security.

Evangelicals did split over separation of families at the border during the 2010s, with Falwell and evangelist Paula White breaking with the group to endorse the practice. Still, alarm bells regarding immigration continued to ring in Evangelical circles.

Tompkins is painfully aware of how those loud voices have in many ways poisoned the Evangelical well when it comes to all kinds of immigrants, be they documented, undocumented, or legally sanctioned refugees. But she sits up straight on her couch as she lets me in on a bright little secret: Despite a lot of public Evangelical opposition to helping strangers in this strange land of ours, there's a whole subculture of far-right Evangelicals offering under-the-table support, away from public view and shielded from political backlash.

Casas was at one time a member of the Southern Baptist Convention, which in 2023, while urging humane treatment of immigrants, nevertheless urged the federal government "to prioritize measures that secure our borders and to provide adequate resources to border patrol and those working in the immigration system."

"I visit a lot of very conservative Tucson-area churches," Tompkins tells me, "and many of them are very good about financially supporting us. But rarely do we get any volunteers from them."

Occasionally, she adds, a breakthrough may occur when she convinces a strongly anti-refugee Evangelical Christian to accompany her to a TRM event.

"There was a woman from an extremely conservative church," she recalls. "I brought her to our center, and I introduced her to a sweet mamma from Sudan.

"They started up a conversation, and I could see the lightbulb going off in her eyes. She was thinking, 'Oh, my gosh! We have commonalities. We both love our families. We both love our cultures and our foods. And we can talk about these things and just be fellow human beings.'

"I think it changed her. Meeting people where they are can make all the difference in the world."

The key may be, Tompkins says (in the most Arizona way imaginable) to separate Evangelical immigration hardliners from their herds, so they can meet people utterly unlike them, yet ultimately human.

"I think the most tragic form of Christian groupthink was the Crusades," Tompkins says. "Some leaders wanted to flex their political arm, and they got all the Christians to buy into the idea of going and killing a bunch of people just to take some land. It really wasn't about Jesus. But the leadership got everyone to *think* it was about Jesus."

We're witnessing echoes of that long-ago power grab now, she says.

"But you can approach Christians individually, away from the group, and show them the hand of Jesus at work in people's lives."

One approach to softening fellow conservative Evangelicals' hearts towards immigrants of all kinds, she adds, is in appealing to their shared Pro-Life positions.

"I don't believe that we should have abortion, because I think that is killing life," she says. "It's killing God's creation. But I also don't believe that we shouldn't let people into the United States. This isn't ours. God owns all of this. I don't know, it's just really weird."

***

As this chapter progresses, you may notice a frustrating lack of voices from Evangelical church members who emphatically support the most severe of national immigration policies, yet who have sought out a common ground when it comes to caring for immigrants as people while they are still here. And believe me, I've tried to get them—particularly among members of a group called Evangelical Immigration Table (EIT), which started during the Obama Administration. It feels as if they fear being boxed in; as if compassion toward undocumented immigrants would require a demand for open borders...or support of strong borders somehow obligates them to endorse harsh treatment of those who've come to this country out of sheer desperation.

The list of charter EIT leaders and organizations—each one seeking to agree upon key principles regarding immigration—is a Holy Who's Who of the Evangelical movement: The National Association of Evangelicals, the Council for Christian Colleges, Focus on the Family, World Vision, Dallas megachurch pastor Tony Evans, and nearly 200 more.

In 2019, these Evangelical powerhouses agreed upon a set of principles that, according to their website, at least, remains fundamentally intact today:

As evangelical Christian leaders, we call for a bipartisan solution on immigration that: Respects the God-given dignity of every person...Protects the unity of the immediate family...Respects the rule of law...guarantees secure national borders...Ensures fairness to taxpayers...Establishes a path toward legal status and/or citizenship for those who qualify and who wish to become permanent residents.

David Drum

I have no reason to doubt members of EIT are diligently pursuing those goals. But as I write this, every e-mail I've sent to the EIT—using a form on their own website—has gone unanswered. And there have been two types of responses when I've approached churches listed as participating congregations on the EIT website: Either stony silence or a polite note saying no, they are not affiliated with EIT. Not anymore, anyway.

The New Testament casts as one of its great earthly villains the Jewish Pharisees—men who made a great show of their so-called virtuous gestures while being anything but charitable in their private lives. In some ways, many of today's Evangelicals resemble an inverse model of that: When it comes to caring for immigrants, legally here or not, they seem content knowing God sees what they're doing in private, while avoiding outward appearances of charity. They're hiding their light of Christian charity under a bushel not out of humility, but due to a perceived sense of self-preservation.

So, that has left me to conclude—somewhat benevolently, I think—that a whole lot of Evangelical churches, while quietly pursuing charitable activities toward immigrants, just don't want the hassle of having to explain themselves to the powerful political forces that might otherwise oppose them.

I spend a good ten minutes walking around the main building at Tucson's Grace to the Nations Church, trying to find the entrance to the staff offices. It doesn't occur to me to head down a flight of stairs to the basement doors—until I see the smiling face of pastor David Drum, holding one open and gesturing me inside.

The underground access to Drum's office seems appropriate for a man who's spent much of his career trying to subvert the unfortunate bonds of faith and politics. Thirteen years ago, he convened six local church leaders—three leaning Republican and three leaning Democratic—and tried to get them to acknowledge that there were social concepts with which they might not be comfortable, but which they would have to agree were legitimately Biblical.

"I created a list called 'Elephant Favorites and Donkey Favorites That Jesus Probably Likes,'" says Drum, a cheerful man with a graying beard, sitting comfy in his windowless office.

The Elephant, or Republican, favorites: Protecting Religious Liberty, Advocating Pro-life Actions on Behalf of the Unborn, and Protecting Marriage.

The Donkey, or Democratic, favorites: Caring for Those Experiencing Poverty, Advocating Pro-life Actions on Behalf of Immigrants and Refugees, and Promoting Racial Equality.

Drum didn't ask the pastors to automatically buy into each other's "favorites." All he sought was the beginning of a dialogue between them.

"That group still meets, thirteen years later," Drum says. "And they still don't agree on everything. But the point is, you can make a strong argument for Biblical support for three things Republicans champion, and also for three things that Democrats champion. So, we ought to be championing all of them. And meeting the needs of immigrants is one of them."

If Evangelicals weren't so bitterly divided over party identity, Drum believes, the nation would have solved the immigration problem a long time ago.

"Evangelical Christians make up a huge part of both liberal and conservative groups," he says. "If we all declared, 'We're not playing that division game anymore,' then I think we would make a lot of progress."

Drum—whose book *Peace Talks: The Good News of Jesus in a Donkey Elephant War*, explores the social rifts among Evangelical Christians—is working to unite churches on the things he believes Evangelicals can agree on.

He gestures to a somewhat sketchy-looking white board hanging on a wall behind me, listing various groups around the nation. The heading reads "J17 Ministries," referencing the chapter of John's Gospel in which Jesus prays for the unity of believers. J17—a loose affiliation of Evangelical believers—is Drum's baby; an attempt to unite churches and other faith groups in finding common ground in the care of immigrants and refugees and then acting on it.

The board lists member groups in Wisconsin, Salt Lake City, Ohio, and Phoenix. There are national strategic teams, even collaborators in Pakistan, France, Switzerland and the United Kingdom.

"All over the country," he says, "we hear hopeful stories of faith-based people, Christian people, all united around the importance of welcoming the stranger, caring for the refugees and displaced people."

The principal conundrum facing Drum and J17 is the persistence of external forces that seem determined to drive wedges between Evangelicals who genuinely want to help those less fortunate than they are.

"Within my own ministry," he says, with a hint of continued surprise, "I've got people who are financial supporters of J17—who were also at Trump's inauguration, because they think he's the greatest thing since sliced bread. And I've got other supporters who are at anti-Trump demonstrations every weekend, all over the country."

Again, there's that caveat: Right-wing "financial" supporters, seemingly cowed into invisibility because of America's radically stratified political climate.

"A whole lot of Evangelical churches lean toward quietism," he says with a sigh. "That means we don't talk about any issue that has political overtones. It's too risky; it's too divisive. I can't count how many times I've heard that, as if preaching the Gospel has no implication for the immigrant family or anybody else in need—that all we care about is punching their ticket to Heaven. It's almost as if when Jesus prayed, 'Thy Kingdom come on Earth as it is in Heaven,' He didn't really mean that."

At the other end of the spectrum, he says, is a kind of syncretism—a blend of political religion and Christianity. And Evangelicals of all stripes can fall into that trap.

"For them," he says, "the political lens has become so strong they can't even tell they've blocked out everything else. It breaks my heart."

The lens of politics, Drum suspects, tends to focus on favored—or disfavored—subjects and magnifies them as essential articles of faith.

"There are lots of Evangelicals who assume the Bible talks a whole lot more about abortion and homosexuality than it does talking about immigrants," he adds. "Well, I have what I would consider Biblically conservative values on abortion and homosexuality, but if we're going to weigh the number of verses addressing those issues, let me tell you it's not even close."

Jeff Simons

If you were making a movie about immigration activists, and if you were to cast a character actor in the part of The Guy Who Runs the Community Center for Immigrants and Refugees, you would definitely look for a guy like Jeff Simons, a man with the casual demeanor of the coolest teacher you ever had; a guy whose head of unkempt, slightly graying hair signifies one for whom vanity is a never-used word from the back end of the dictionary; a soft-spoken friend-of-everyone in a plaid shirt and loose jeans.

"Come on in!" he says with a welcoming wave, ushering me from the beating sun of a Tucson neighborhood through the door of a former church hall. Inside there is a rustle of hushed activity: Five minority high school students are huddled at individual tables with after-school tutors, part of a mentoring program sponsored by the Tucson Refugee Ministry.

Elsewhere in the room I spot a jumble of donated clothing. "Sorry for the mess," says Simons, "We're just starting that program and we haven't sorted things yet."

Simons recently inherited the ministry's executive director position from Jennifer Tompkins—until now he's been largely responsible for the group's Arrive and Thrive initiative.

Twice a week, Simons hosts a community coffee shop in this room, welcoming anyone from the immigrant community, whether they are taking their first, tentative, steps of assimilation or seeking to further establish themselves in the local society.

"We have a workforce development program here," Simons says, "so we can help people find jobs."

He introduces me to Anna, a young staff member who moved from

Kentucky to study at the University of Arizona and who stumbled upon Tucson Refugee Ministries while participating in a TRM campus-based outreach project.

"TRM was holding what they call a family picnic," she tells me. "Really, what that meant was we just brought pizza to an apartment complex that had lots of refugees living there. I got to meet people, and learn their stories, and I just fell in love with it."

Simons lifts from a low table a photo of a tall, smiling young man. He chuckles.

"Oh, this is great," he says. "This just happened, like, two hours ago. He's named Khalifa, and he's a refugee from Sudan. He had experience painting cars, so we've just helped him get a job at Jim Click Autos here in Tucson."

Simons leads me toward a door at the far end of the large room.

"So," he says without irony, "you have just seen the sexiest part of our place. Now I'll show you the rest of it."

We pass through a door to a modest playground, where for four Tuesdays each June TRM sponsors an international Kids Camp, offering food and activities for upwards of eighty children of newcomers. In a classroom-like space facing the square is a sewing and craft room, where immigrant women create items of clothing.

"We get a lot of material donations for this," he says. "And then, about four times a year, we host an artisans' market where they can sell their stuff and keep whatever they make."

Finally—and perhaps, to Simons' mind, most significantly—there's a room where TRM sponsors English as a Second Language (ESL) classes.

"For so many people, especially the older ones, the language barrier is such a struggle," he says. "The younger people, they get it. They arrive and they know, 'I gotta learn English.' And they'll immediately get on YouTube and get to work.

"But the older folks, I don't know, they just seem to want to hold on to their old language. It doesn't help that they haven't had much education, so they've never learned how to learn.

"A guy told me, 'I never went to school. I can't learn.' So, we do individual tutoring, and volunteers will go to their houses to help out."

He leans against a wall.

"So," he says, "that's the big tour."

For Simons, the road to this modest oasis of faith-based benevolence has been more than a little twisty. Born in Fresno, California, he taught in

Orange County where he married and had kids. For a long time, he taught ESL to adults—a job he loved above all others.

"It's the purest kind of teaching," Simons says, his eyes alight. "I taught high school and junior high for a while, and a whole lot of those kids just don't want to be there. It's just so hard to make them apply themselves.

"But adults—it's all voluntary. No coercion or obligation. I fell in love with those people."

So deep was Simons' newfound connection to the immigrant community, in fact, that he got a master's degree in intercultural studies. After participating in a series of short-term Evangelical Christian missionary trips, in 2005 he and his wife packed up their things and moved with two young children to Oaxaca, Mexico. There they stayed for fourteen years, living with indigenous people high in the mountains.

A 2019 furlough to Southern California was rendered permanent by COVID-19. Lured to Tucson by reports of the work of TRM, he briefly taught English there before signing on as the group's latest chief executive.

TRM has a staff of about ten people, and if you think that sounds like too few bodies to get too much done, you're right—and that's by design.

"The point isn't really for us to run the coffee shop, and teach the classes, and help people find jobs," he says. "Our job is to inspire and enlist the people of the church, the Body of Christ, to get involved in our work."

Among Arizona Evangelicals, he estimates, roughly half support the spirit of the group's mission.

"There are some who disagree with the government's attitude toward immigrants and refugees, who believe working with the stranger or the foreigner is just a Biblical thing they should be doing," he says. "And they tend to participate in what we're doing.

"Those who agree with the government tend not to be involved with us at all."

Still, he adds, he has seen more than one Evangelical heart softened by an encounter with actual immigrants.

"I have a buddy," he says, "definitely a Republican, definitely in agreement with the administration on a lot of things, and we went down to Mexico for a guys' weekend together, just to hang out."

Simons did have one side trip planned, though: He took his friend for a visit to a settlement of Haitian refugees who'd run into the brick wall of U.S. immigration policy; eighty-five people living in tents with one kitchen and a couple of bathrooms.

"That opened his eyes," Simons recalls. "Sometimes you just have to meet people, and hear their stories, and experience their sheer humanity. Then you get an entirely new perspective. You begin to understand—and this is true especially for Christians—that it's our responsibility, maybe even our privilege, to take care of the stranger and the foreigner in our midst.

"It's crystal clear. And yet, somehow, some people don't see that."

Simons guides me back to the front door, and I step into the afternoon Tucson sun. As I walk to my car, I cast my gaze up and down the street, taking in the neighborhood's modest homes, ranging from small houses to single-level duplexes. I contemplate the people behind many of those doors, too frightened to step into this same sunlight.

It's no way for people to live, I think. And no way to ask them to.

Brian Conway in the field

Southeastern Arizona: Cut-and-Dry Realities

When the Wells Go Kerflooey, Party Differences Wither

I know I've got to move on from Arizona. Too many more chapters based here and I'll have to find a new title for the book.

But I'm compelled to stay a couple more days after seeing the photo I have sitting on my dashboard. The shot at first seems an odd composition: A sunglassed man, standing near a dirt road, with mountains in the distance, posing next to a telephone pole.

"Near Willcox, Arizona," reads a placard attached to the pole.

Posted on the pole, a body height above the man's head, is the designation "11.5 feet," and above that, "1969."

The man in the photo is Brian Conway, the principal hydrogeologist for Arizona's Department of Water Resources. The photo dramatizes, in the most graphic manner imaginable, a chilling truth: In the course of fifty-five years, the land on this lonely stretch of road has sunk farther than the depth of an Olympic swimming pool.

Conway periodically drives out to the spot to update the steady downward progression of this valley floor. The cause of its precipitous drop? Excessive pumping of groundwater to support an explosion of agriculture near Willcox.

In other words, the good people of Willcox found their aquifer wet and fat, like a just-used kitchen sponge. Over the past century or so, they have been wringing it dry.

Willcox sits in a sandy valley about ninety miles east of Tucson. Just to its south, dust whirls like cartoon Tasmanian Devils across the parched 40-square-mile expanse of the Willcox Playa, a dry lakebed.

When it comes to water supply, the State of Arizona tends to look at its southeastern corner and give a jaunty wave of "Good luck!" No rivers flow through nor empty into the region's landscape; there are absolutely no plans to ever plow an aqueduct here like the one that saved Tucson. For centuries, the watery whims of nature were barely enough to sustain the few hundred residents who ran small family farms or ranched the surrounding land or worked for the railroad that ran through town.

Then came mega-agriculture.

And by far the most land-grabbing—and water-gobbling—area resident is Riverview Dairy.

Pull up a Google satellite view of Willcox and its environs, and besides the sandy, ear-shaped outline of Willcox Playa, the dominant feature, to the southeast, is a twenty-mile-long swath of circular, center-pivot irrigation fields resembling a vast game board covered with green checkers. This is the waterlogged realm of Riverview, a Minnesota-based conglomerate that, at last report, owns 37,000 acres in Willcox with 75,000 cattle and plans for 75,000 more. To feed all those chomping cuds, the company grows corn, wheat and alfalfa, hurling an acre-feet of water into the air, counting on what does not evaporate in the dry desert air to moisten their crops.

The evaporation rate is astronomical.

But there is little incentive on Riverview's part to save water because, under longtime Arizona law, groundwater is basically free for the taking. Fairly or not, to the minds of most people who live in and around Willcox, Riverview represents the main reason their land is currently riding a down escalator. Even among conservatives who once railed against government regulation (and still do, in non-water-related areas), the cry from southeastern Arizona is: "Enough."

***

On East Maley Street In downtown Willcox, I spot a bumper sticker that reads: "Riverview Sucks (Every Drop of OUR Water!")

The sticker and the car attached to it belong to Sharon Hill, owner of The Friendly Bookstore.

"All we have is the ground water," says Hill. "It's fossil water; left here several ice ages ago. And it's sinking fast."

Hill and her husband live four miles north of town on a ten-acre farm.

"Our residential pump is producing about a quart of water an hour," Sharon says. "Luckily, we can haul water from the residential well on our nephew's farm next door, which has been allowed to go fallow."

Others are not so lucky. In the grocery store, Sharon says, she overhears local people whispering to each other about running illicit water lines from one neighbor's house to another. More than 300 area residents, she says, must now haul water from downtown to their far-flung homes after an outlying municipal well "went kerflooey."

In Willcox, that snorkeling sound you hear is that of a thousand straws sucking up the last drops from the bottom of a drinking glass.

Land subsidence due to falling water levels is having more immediately visible consequences, as well.

"I know a woman north of town; the foundation of her house cracked, and now the house is sitting there lopsided," Sharon says. "And there's not much people can do to fix these things; a quarter of us here live below the poverty level."

As you might expect from the New Jersey-born owner of a new-and-used book store, Sharon can be stridently liberal. But she says the people of Willcox—who number overwhelmingly in the conservative column—have had an epiphany regarding the need for some sort of regulation when it comes to water use.

As a prime example, she points to Bill Curry, a longtime area farmer and owner of Curry Seed and Chile Co., just south of the Willcox Playa.

A staunch conservative in the Arizona mold, Curry grew up in the valley his family has farmed since 1952. Although water was just about free, it was hard to get to deep underground, and the aquifer levels varied from decade to decade. The Currys didn't waste the precious resource, and their conservative roots resisted any government attempts to regulate its use. The market, conservative farmers argued, was the aquifer's friend. If the price of corn, cotton, or alfalfa dropped, so did the number of acres farmed, and thus, so did water use. During those periods, the aquifer had a chance to replenish itself.

"I've seen it three times in my life," Bill Curry—who frequently speaks to farming groups but rarely sits down for interviews—told *The Arizona Republic* in 2024.

Abandoned water well near Willcox

But that was before water-guzzling Riverview Dairy moved in. And then came pecan farmers, whose trees drank from the aquifer like a kid sucking down a Happy Meal Coke. Perhaps ironically, that profligate use of water on the part of industrial farming was the main reason Curry opposed a 2020 ballot initiative to create an Active Management Area around Willcox—limiting farmers to their average water use for the previous five years. The regulation meant that conservation-conscious Curry—who had already invested in expensive water-saving technology like drip irrigation, and who had planted half his property with low water-use crops like rosemary and cacti—would face severe water limitations while the big boys continued to splash around water like sparrows in a bird bath.

Arizona has imposed a freeze on additional levels of water use, and while Curry still doesn't like the idea of the state dictating water policy, he's happy to align with liberal environmentalists, visiting farmer groups to advocate for local measures to preserve water.

"We'll handle it ourselves and we'll control it," he told Arizona Attorney General Kris Mayes in February, 2024. "We'll solve it. That's the kind of people we are."

In October 2023, many were surprised when Curry, a frequent critic of the state, stepped in to fill a vacancy on the Arizona governor's Water Policy Council. Curry continues to defend local farmers against what he sees as draconian levels of control—but he does so with an eye on crafting compromise legislation that can work for everyone.

According to reports, Curry can be a fiery advocate, but he also understands both sides of the discussion are trying to preserve Arizona's way of life. He makes it a point to refer to regulation-minded council members as "fine people," and at a March, 2024 Arizona legislature hearing regarding a bill that would have created a state-mandated "basin management area" at Willcox, Curry offered a humbling apology to Rep. Gail Griffin, publicly regretting an altercation they'd had earlier.

"I personally want to apologize to you, Gail," Curry said. "I got too ugly, and you know it and I know it. We can't work that way."

***

As I wander Sharon Hill's bookstore, looking for anything she might have on Willcox's water history, she reaffirms her admiration for Curry, a man with whom she shares little common ground.

"He's just a very wise, eloquent man," she tells me.

I buy a book from Sharon: a 1964 volume called *Southwestern Town: The Story of Willcox, Arizona*. The slim volume relates the early history of Chiricahua people here, and the marauding Spaniards, the era of open range ranching, the arrival of the Southern Pacific Railroad, the beginning of copper mining in the nearby mountains—the excitement over an oil discovery that turned out to be seepage from a railroad storage tank.

On page thirty-three is a dramatic photo of downtown Willcox under several feet of floodwater. The year is 1905, a time when apparently the main local concern regarding water was too much of it.

"At lots of our community meetings, people still say our main problem is the drought," says Sharon. "But the climate is changing, and we don't know if the drought will ever end."

She gestures out the window, across the street, toward the creeping sands of Willcox Playa.

"That underground water is six million years old," she says. "Even if we all disappeared tomorrow, the Department of Water Resources tells us it would be 300 years before the aquifer got recharged. I'm glad there are people like me worried about it. And I'm glad there are people like Bill Curry who are trying to do something about it."

I'm finally done with Arizona. As I drive away from Willcox, I think of Brian Conway's land elevation yardstick, and how it will never see the desert surface creep back toward its 1969 levels. Willcox's underground water storage space is gone for good.

***

And so, at best those working to head off continued excess water usage under Willcox are, by definition, exclusively in the business of damage control.

"The majority of people here are concerned," hydrogeologist Conway says. "They want to do something about it."

And as they say at Alcoholics Anonymous, in addressing a whole other kind of drinking issue, agreeing there's a problem is the first step toward actually making a difference.

Renee Miller & Jill Finke

Brenham, Texas: Three Lessons from a Texas Town

The Power of Shared Histories

Lesson 1: The Best Chili Has More Than One Kind of Bean

Vintage Southern Comfort Bed and Breakfast sits at the quiet corner of Park and Axer Streets in Brenham, Texas, a crossroads ranch town settled by German immigrants in the mid-1800s. The eighty-year-old house is typical of the neighborhood: a single-story wood frame with a cozy front porch swing. At night you can curl up there and eavesdrop on the hooting conversation between two Great Horned Owls, perched on the swaying boughs of twin crepe myrtles flanking the concrete sidewalk.

Renee Mueller and Jill Finke are waiting for me on that porch when I arrive in midafternoon (I'd originally figured I'd drive here from Tucson via Interstate 10, forgetting that although Arizona and Texas nearly bump against each other, it's still a 1,000-mile slog). The sisters bought this house for their aging mother years ago, and after her passing in 2016, they converted it into a guest house.

"We didn't plan to," says Jill, "but then we looked at our property tax bill and figured we'd better do something with it."

Renee and Jill grew up next door to this house, about four blocks from Brenham's business district. From where the sisters sit, it's just a short walk to the tree-shaded gazebo bandstand behind the limestone Washington County Courthouse.

Aside from a period around the Civil War when the railroad came through and launched the town into a bustling business center, for the better part of two centuries, Brenham has slumbered in relative anonymity, nestled in Washington County, a no man's land roughly halfway between Austin and Houston. (Still, the town has exported an impressive variety of favorite sons and daughters, including legendary blues singer Blind Willie Jackson, pioneer African American photographer Louise Martin, and radio bad boy Don Imus.)

But now the cities are coming to call. Like great trees adding rings each year, the metropolitan areas of Houston and Austin are relentlessly pushing their boundaries in Brenham's direction.

Starting about twenty years ago, Houstonians and Austinians alike have discovered in Brenham—with its Mayberry downtown, dusty antique shops and sprouting vineyards—a likely place to set down weekend roots. When COVID-19 informed the world that you could work from just about anywhere you wanted (at least until the bosses got fed up), a lot of those weekend retreats morphed into full-time residences with tax write-off office spaces.

And so now, the bedrock families of Brenham, many of them custodians of a century or more of conservative tradition, find themselves increasingly sharing their storefronts, restaurants and schoolrooms with transplants from two of Texas' bluest of blue metropolitan areas.

But here's the thing many non-Texans don't get: Despite what you may have heard about the state's bitter social divide, in Brenham everyone seems totally okay with it.

"I don't even know how some of my friends vote," says my server at The Tilted Windmill, a wide-open dining space on Commerce Street. "Why get into something that's just going to stir up stuff?"

I am listening to her words, but I can't take my widening eyes off my plate. This morning's Tilted Windmill house breakfast specialty is calling me. The menu identifies it as French Toast, but it's really a long, braided donut topped with strawberry compote and whipped cream. A dejected sausage patty sits alongside, having utterly given up on drawing any attention to itself. I have immediately come to understand why everyone here seems to soak in peaceful coexistence: How could any interpersonal conflicts exist in a place where Tilted Windmill French Toast exists?

But there is, my server adds, another ingredient in the get-along mix:

"One thing about Texas…" she adds. "We're all pretty independent, no matter what our politics are. You're not going to change anyone's mind about anything. So why try?"

***

Ironically, it seems that Texans' notorious independent streak may be the very thing that enables them to mingle convivially among those with whom they disagree—at times bitterly. It's in their history.

Texas was, of course, a Confederate state, but rather than dwell on that unfortunate alliance, you'll find that Texans would much rather focus on the days when Texas was, in every sense of the word, an independent and sovereign nation.

I don't know about you, but growing up in the Great Northeast I may have heard vague stories about The Texas Republic and the Texas War of Independence, but I'd always chalked that talk up to Chamber of Commerce boosterism meant to rationalize Texans' stubborn go-it-alone-if-necessary spirit.

"We are the only state that could secede if we wanted to," my B&B host Renee Mueller tells me. That's a popular conception among Texans—although the last time Texas tried it, a lot of people died and Texas still ended up as one star among many on the U.S. flag. That said, the fact that the notion of secession still swells the hearts of Texans—and not those of, say, similarly independent-minded Vermonters—illustrates how jealously Lone Star Staters proclaim their individuality, no matter what their political backgrounds.

Aside from maybe Hawaiians—who celebrate their pre-U.S. culture with unsurpassed fervor—it would be hard to name a state population as thoroughly wrapped up in their unique historical past as Texans. Six Flags, you may not know, is not just the name of a theme park in Houston; it details the six separate flags that have flown over the state's territory: Spain, France, Mexico, The Texas Republic, the Confederacy and the United States. What's more, each of the transitions those flags represent involved not a little battle and bloodshed. So, while it may or may not be true that Texas can leave the United States any old time it wants to, the notion of pulling away, of resisting perceived unjust authority, is pretty much baked into the chili here.

It's not a liberal or conservative thing. It's a Texas thing.

Lloyd Powell

Lesson 2: Everybody Wants to Feel Safe

They must teach police academy cadets how to knock on a door in a way that is guaranteed to get the attention of whomever is on the other side of it. As I putter around the kitchen of the Vintage Southern Comfort Bed & Breakfast, there comes at the front a rapid, machine gun-like pounding that for some reason has me glancing around to make sure there's no incriminating evidence lying about.

The pounding stops. I stride toward the door. The pounding starts up again, just as urgent. I swing the door open, expecting to find a SWAT team wielding a battering ram.

Instead, I find the smiling, bearded-yet-cherubic face of Lloyd Powell, for twenty-eight years a police officer in Brenham and, since March 2024, its police chief.

Across the street, I think I see a neighbor in their doorway watching the town's top cop encounter a transient stranger. I put on the broadest, goofiest smile I can muster, just for her benefit.

"You really know how to knock on a door," I say as I welcome Powell inside. He laughs, and I immediately feel like he's the type of guy who laughs easily. We head for the dining room table, and I duck into the kitchen to make coffee on the B&B Keurig machine I've just figured out how to use. Tossing conversation from room to room, we share our backstories.

Powell was born and raised in Brenham, and left only to get his education in Louisiana at Grambling State University.

"I've literally spent my entire law enforcement career right here," he says, gesturing toward the street beyond the front porch. "If you're gonna risk your life for somebody, why not make it somebody you know?"

I should mention that Powell is Black; the first African American chief in Brenham's history—understandable, because police chiefs around here tend to settle in for life, and for long lives, at that: His predecessor passed away just five months after retiring. Powell considered him a mentor and a friend.

Virtually every police official in the country will tell you that law enforcement should be colorblind; that officers should apply law enforcement equally, with no consideration for the race of the citizens they encounter. But that memo, Powell says, has not been received by many of those people police are trying to protect.

"I talk to a lot of people in my community, the Black community, who don't like the police, no matter what the color of the police officer is," Powell says as I return from the kitchen. "It's a difficult conversation to have, but one we need to have anyway."

He accepts a cup of coffee and wraps his hands around it.

"Here's an example," he says. "I was at a local high school football game, in uniform, and I saw a fella I knew talking with another guy—and I could tell from the moment I walked up to them that guy was uncomfortable.

"I looked at him and said, 'Hey, how you doing?' And he just looks down and says, 'You know, I don't like cops.'"

Powell glances up; we're eye-to-eye for a second, and in his expression, I can see his unspoken, incredulous thought: "*Why would anybody not like me*?"

Returning to his story, Powell recalls asking the man if he'd had bad experiences with the police. Powell, naturally, knew the answer: *Of course he had.*

"I said, 'I'm sorry for that. Was it me?' He said no, it wasn't. And he smiled. And I know from experience if you can make someone smile, you can start a real conversation."

Powell stood there in his police uniform, listening. He didn't make any excuses for that abrasive cop. He didn't ask why he'd gotten into the confrontation in the first place. It didn't take long—just a few minutes—for the man to get talked out on the subject.

"So, we started to talk about football," says Powell, his eyes twinkling. "It took a little bit of time, but finally I saw a lightbulb come on in his head: 'Oh, yeah. He's a regular person.'"

But why, I ask, do police get painted with such a broad, angry brush? If the waiter in a restaurant is rude to me, I don't say, "Well, I'm never going to trust another restaurant because that waiter was a jerk."

Powell politely smiles and shakes his head, but I can tell he's wondering why, when he arrived, he didn't see the turnip truck that I fell off parked outside.

"A waiter can't *kill* you," he says.

I can tell Powell has never eaten at some of the places I have in Midtown Manhattan, but his point is well-taken.

"A waiter can't even deprive you of your freedom on a moment's notice," he continues. "And a waiter doesn't have a gun."

Well, hold on, I interject: We're in Texas. Not only could a waiter have a gun; in all likelihood, even the kid at the McDonald's drive-up is packing right now.

He has to agree with me.

"True," he chuckles. "But my point is, everybody just wants to feel safe. They want to feel protected. When someone doesn't feel safe—if it's the police officer or if it's the citizen—that's when things can go wrong."

Of course, people don't generally pay their taxes so they can feel like they're protecting their police force. Most folks consider that protection thing a one-way street, and Powell doesn't have a problem with that.

"I put the onus on law enforcement," he says. "It takes a lot of work to go out and encounter people; to go to schools and community groups just to talk with them. But you just have to do it; you have to encounter people in situations that can't possibly end up with you putting them in jail."

Powell concedes that it's easy to get spoiled in laid-back Brenham.

"The people here embrace their law enforcement," he says. "Maybe because they see how things are over in Austin and Houston, where in some cases people feel like the police are an occupying force."

Sure, I say, it's easy to forge positive relationships with law-abiding citizens; the ones you run into at ball games and civic club meetings. But cops, by definition, encounter society's criminal element daily. That, I suggest, must surely strain the "let's sit down and talk" approach to law enforcement.

Or maybe not.

"I worked narcotics for ten years," he says. "I worked out relationships with criminals and drug dealers and gang members. They're still people. Yeah, they chose a bad lot in life, but I wouldn't treat a gang member any differently than I'm treating you right now, so long as they give me the opportunity to be nice to them."

There are, of course, more than a few knuckleheads out there who aren't willing to give Powell, or anyone in uniform, that chance.

He calls them his "Fan Club."

"It's a pretty large club," he says with a laugh. "Some people who just hate me. People you can't sway.

"But I can only be me. If you break the law and you don't recognize the fact that you're going to have to deal with the consequences, then, yeah, you've got a problem there. And I'll try to talk you through it, if you'll let me."

Powell's conciliatory approach to law enforcement may well have been honed during his years as a hostage negotiator—a skill that can occasionally become necessary even in a low-key town like Brenham.

"That was so much fun," he says, and he laughs at my uncomprehending stare.

Fun?

"Oh, yeah," he enthuses. "Let me tell you, if you want to learn how to find your common denominator with someone—with anyone—approach it like a hostage negotiator."

The key, he explains, is to look beyond the current crisis—which is almost certainly the most stressful moment of the person's life—and try to normalize things by finding something else to talk about.

"When you walk into a hostage situation," he explains, "you have to find out who this person is. We talk a little bit. What does he like? What doesn't he like?

"We might talk about dogs for thirty minutes. You got a dog? Yeah, I got a dog, too. A Cane Corso. Oh, I like those. And so, this guy and I have ninety-nine ways in which we're different—but I found the one thing we have in common."

From that germ of similarity, Powell says, a true relationship can be built.

"He sees I'm a regular person—and I see he's a regular person, despite what he's going through right now. We can start talking about the things we want; the things we don't want. And from there we can talk about what each of us wants, and what each of us doesn't want."

Powell gives me a moment to let all this sink in. He knows what I'm

Trey Holleway

here to talk with him about, and he can sense I'm already piecing together his larger point.

America, he says, just might need a hostage negotiator.

"Just like the cop on the outside who wants one thing, and the hostage taker inside who wants another thing, this country has taken sides," he says. This country has to develop rapport again. We need to quit treating our politics as if we're on opposing teams."

The same thing, he says, goes for race relations. Powell, fifty, a Black man who grew up in rural Texas, believes America's race divide is the worst he's ever seen.

"Just like some people say, 'We can't be friends because you're Red and I'm Blue,' the same thing sometimes translates to race. You're here or you're there. You're Black or you're white.

"Instead of focusing on our differences, we need to look at the things we have in common. And it's not hard to find them."

Lesson Three: Don't Play in Boxes

About a half-hour after Chief Powell and I say our goodbyes, another knock comes on the door. Prepared this time for that distinctive "Open up or we'll break the door down" clatter, I calmly open it to find the smiling face of Trey Holleway, the recently elected sheriff for this part of Washington County. Parked at the curb is his Sheriff's Department patrol vehicle, and beyond that, again, I think I see the outline of that neighbor in the doorway. I give a jaunty, self-conscious wave in that general direction.

Sitting across from me, it's easy to see Holleway has all the esthetics you'd want in a candidate for sheriff: Tall, rugged, trimmed beard, easy smile, piercing blue eyes. Today he's in a baseball cap, but I've seen campaign photos of Holleway in a black felt cowboy hat, and for an Easterner like me, it is easy to imagine him galloping down Brenham's Alamo Street, Colt 45 raised, chasing the varmints who just robbed the Brenham National Bank.

Holleway was born in Washington County, and has never roamed far from home: His thirty-plus years in law enforcement include time with the Capitol Police in nearby Austin, as a Texas State trooper, and as a criminal investigator. He's a big believer in "perceptual vigilance": being aware of your surroundings and avoiding behaviors that can make you susceptible to criminal attacks. ("I love my wife's beautiful ponytail, but if she's out walking by herself, she needs to tuck that thing away. Bad guys love to pull at ponytails.")

Still, from a law enforcement viewpoint, Holleway says it's dangerous to generalize just who "bad guys" are. He knows police across the country are seen as entering perilous situations with pre-conceived notions of who the bad guys are going to be, but he also insists that kind of attitude is self-defeating for cops.

"What aggravates me personally is this tendency for humans to put other humans in a box," he says. "As a law enforcement officer, I've got to see you first as a fellow human being. I'm going to treat you with respect, no matter how you treat me. When we put people in boxes, we lose sight of who we truly are."

But there's another perspective to the "box" issue, he says: Due to the long, often turbulent history of citizens and police, an awful lot of people presuppose that they have been placed in a box by law enforcement when, in reality, they have not. And that outlook colors their expectations and subsequent interactions with officers.

"I'm a professional," Holleway says. "It's my job to try hard and not see people that way. But when people think you've put them in a box, they tend to believe the box is real. It is part of the job of law enforcement professionals to convince people that those boxes are not real. That people are seen for who they are."

Holleway approaches this outlook from a particularly personal aspect: He and his wife Laurie, already the parents of two kids, adopted two Black children, a girl and a boy, from Houston.

"In the end," he says softly, "after we'd spent a good deal of time just trying to determine who their parents were, we were unable to do that. So, we adopted them."

The Holleways provided their new children with a loving home bristling with opportunities that, just months earlier, had seemed unthinkable for them. But the couple never harbored fantasies of their new arrivals automatically adapting to their new surroundings, like goldfish newly arrived from a pet store.

"It's an understatement to say they came from an environment that didn't have a positive view of law enforcement," he says. "Where they come from, nearly every encounter with law enforcement was negative. And then, all of a sudden, here are these two white people, one of whom is a cop, saying 'We love you just the way you are, for who you are.'"

Holleway pointed his new children to a speech made by Dr. Martin Luther King: "If a man is called to be a street sweeper…he should sweep streets so well that all the hosts of Heaven and Earth will pause to say, 'Here lived a great street sweeper!"

Holleway recalls, "I reminded them about the lives of Dr. King and Frederick Douglass and Colin Powell. What men they were! And I said, 'If these people could accomplish things like this in the world they were living in, there's nothing to stop you from doing everything you want to in your life.'"

Today Holleway's adopted son is in the Army. His daughter lives in Minnesota with her partner and two children. And they are living precisely the lives they want to live.

"But first," he said, "they had to get out of the box they saw themselves in…and they had to understand that we didn't see them as being in a box, either."

As we wrap up, I congratulate Holleway on winning the recent sheriff's election, against another member of his same department. I wonder aloud if that might have led to some uncomfortable moments at work.

"Oh, no, my opponent's a great guy," he says, "There was no mudslinging. We just both wanted the same job."

I thank Holleway for his time and mention I'm about to walk to the nearest auto rental office to pick up a car. He offers to drive me.

Together, we walk out to his cruiser. As I climb in, I can imagine that neighbor thinking Holleway must have found his man.

Another box.

***

If you listen to the mass media soundtrack chronicling Texas' regular electoral clashes between liberal and conservative candidates—most of which end up favoring the right wing—you'll assume people in the Lone Star State live with a persistent background noise of simmering conflict. But after few days in Brenham, asking gently probing questions and listening to the measured replies, I begin to believe my bed and breakfast co-host, Renee, has boiled the Texas culture clash down to a bluntly basic philosophy:

"I think, in the end, you learn to keep your mouth shut," she says. "Everyone has their own opinions, of course, but you also have to realize what you can and cannot say, especially in public."

She hastens to add that revolving door of keep-it-to-yourself-ness turns both ways: Even when people of one persuasion are in a dominant majority, in small town Texas there's little inclination to beat the minority over the head.

"I think it's a southern thing," she says. "And also a small town thing. In a city, where not everyone knows you, you might be more inclined to say exactly what's on your mind. And although we have a lot of people moving in, we still look and feel like a small town. If you're not related to a bunch of people here, you're probably going to have to work with us, or go to our restaurants and stores.

"In Brenham, and I think in a lot of towns like Brenham, people end up looking beyond their differences and working together for common goals."

How long does it take for those new arrivals from Houston and Austin get the memo?

The sisters smile.

"They catch on pretty quick," says Jill.

***

It's probably fair to say that many people in the U.S. look somewhat askance at Texans' obsession with their national/state history. Certainly, I have. Even though there are family and friends I dearly love in Texas, for decades I have silently wished they would just get over themselves. (This probably has much to do with my attitude toward the Dallas Cowboys.

Still, in Texas there is the germ of something to which we should as a nation, perhaps, aspire. Texans are, in substantial ways, locked in cultural wars regarding education, gender issues, reproductive rights, and permissible weapons. But no matter how far left or right I ventured in Texas, the pride of place among Texans remained unshakeable.

Texas is the size of a medium-sized country. Why can't Americans at large find a way to summon up a similarly fierce devotion to their shared history and heritage as a way to bridge the political and cultural gaps between them? This would probably entail people on the left softening their understandable, but divisive, obsession with seeking reparation for historical social injustice. And those on the right would need to openly acknowledge the reality of systemic injustices, with a willingness to confront them in the here and now.

Or perhaps we could just find parallel things to be proud of: The right takes pride in America's technological and industrial accomplishments; the left sees the compassionate nature of social programs as the height of government accomplishment.

These are not incompatible points of pride. If the good people of Texas can somehow draw together under the banner of state/nationhood, why could not the rest of us?

Mark Irwin

Nashville, Tennessee:

Singing from the Same Hymnbook

A conservative citadel—and a music-fueled political melting pot

Nashville's Ryman Auditorium is called The Mother Church of Country Music for good reason: Every day of every year, the faithful mount its stone steps, reverently slip into its pews, and then just sit there, as if the lights will dim, the curtain will rise, and Hank Williams will step into the spotlight to warble "I Saw the Light."

Some may even be tempted to genuflect as the faint echoes of long-gone Ryman regulars like Patsy Cline or Hank Snow or even the Brinkley Brothers Dixie Clodhoppers whisper in their ears.

It is ungodly cold in Nashville, even for February, as a north wind blows down Fourth Avenue. Outside the auditorium—for thirty years home of The Grand Ole Opry—you'd freeze your lips solid if you were to bend down and kiss the life-sized bronze statue of four-foot ten Opry legend Little Jimmy Dickens. But country music fans, congenitally good-natured, are still happy to pause outside and chat about the uniquely American sound that, perhaps more than any other genre, embraces all corners of the nation's culture.

"I can't say *what* the politics are of my favorite singers," says Pearl, a South Dakota nurse visiting Nashville with her husband, James. "I mean, I assume they think like I do. But I don't know."

She glances at James and laughs, "Maybe I don't want to know!"

Pearl's name, she says, was bestowed on her by long-distance Opry congregant parents who listened to country comedian Minnie Pearl on the Grand Ol Opry radio show—which has aired every week, uninterrupted, for 100 years as of November 2025. Before there was the big bands' *Make Believe Ballroom*, before there was rock and roll's *American Bandstand*, there was country's Grand Ole Opry, beamed nationwide from Nashville's WSM Radio and sponsored, for decades, by Goo Goo Cluster candy.

As if homing in on that beacon of slide guitars and frantic fiddles, for more than a century musicians, singers, and songwriters have converged on Nashville. Conservative, liberal, anarchic and agnostic, that army of creative immigrants has shared one unified vision: To create music that speaks the language of America.

***

"Country music isn't about politics," says Mark Irwin, a longtime Nashville songwriter who has penned hits for Alan Jackson, Tim McGraw, and Taylor Swift, to drop just a few top-tier names.

"It's about a person's place in the world—things that are important to everyone. Things like relationships, and family, and country. It's about a way of life that people can relate to, no matter what their political beliefs."

Irwin and I are standing in the doorway of The Well Coffeehouse on Nashville's 16th Street, more popularly known as Music Row thanks to the recording studios and record companies that line it. We're holding our hot drinks, waiting for a table to open up, to no avail.

"Here, let's just sit up there," he says, gesturing toward a small stage with three chairs and a guitar on it. There are stages everywhere in Nashville; in coffee shops, restaurants, drug stores and even at the airport. In 1992, driving through the city on my way from Washington, DC to Dallas, I stopped at a Denny's just outside of Nashville—and was greeted by a spangle-vested, white cowboy-hatted, leather-booted songstress standing two steps from the register, strumming on her guitar and chirping "Crazy."

Crazy, indeed. The room at The Well quiets just a bit on the off chance a show might be starting. But when neither one of us makes a move for the guitar, the volume pops back to normal.

"In the studio," Irwin says, "it's all about making music. I'd say 99.9 percent of the time, politics stays outside. We might discuss politics to a point, but we really talk guitars. We talk about our life experiences. We talk about the people we love and the world outside. You know; country music stuff."

That's not to say the good music-making people of Nashville are without political or social outlooks. That's never been the case.

Irwin, born in the Bronx and raised in Hackensack, NJ, arrived in Nashville in 1987 at the tail end of an era that was dominated by the likes of Kris Kristofferson and Johnny Cash.

"It was a pretty liberal culture around here at the time, with crazy poets and whatnot," he says.

Irwin's first job was as a dishwasher at the Bluebird Café, a ninety-seat venue that launched the singing careers of Kathy Mattea and Garth Brooks. He soon graduated to bartender, where he became acquainted with Nashville figures, including a young singer named Alan Jackson.

"We became friends," Irwin recalls, "and a few days later we were in a room together, writing a song that changed both of our lives."

The song was "Here in the Real World," a somber, but sprightly meditation on how the rosy expectations engendered by movies and TV can mask the inevitable sorrow of life.

"Here in the Real World" was nominated for Best Song by the Academy of Country Music—somehow twice, in both 1990 and 1991.

In Mark Bego's 1996 biography *Alan Jackson: Gone Country*, Jackson recalls, "I had these opening lines, 'Cowboys don't cry and heroes don't die.' I didn't really know where it was heading...We started hammering away at it. It was about an hour and half later, I guess, when we came out of the office with that song."

That "throw them in an office and see what they come up with" strategy has been a modus operandi in Nashville for decades. More than in perhaps any other entertainment medium, Nashville music publishers like to engage in a sort of creative alchemy, mixing and matching songwriters of varying outlooks and backgrounds. In fact, in a world where creatives seem determined to choose up ideological sides, Nashville's music industry has

Franklin Town Square

found that teaming up writers whose backgrounds and outlooks might otherwise clash can create the kind of artistic tension that strikes sparks of creativity.

Coincidentally, Irwin tells me, just before our meetup he was engaged in just such a chemistry experiment.

"Today I was put together with two people—a woman from Canada, who's very successful, and a guy who, believe it or not, owns a lighting business but is a very good songwriter. It was our first day on this project, so we just talked a lot because we haven't seen each other in a while."

Irwin figures the trio cranked out half a song this morning. "But we're on the same page," he says, meaning they're trying to come up with something that will be of specific interest to one of Nashville's younger generation of stars. "We're trying to get the Jelly Rolls and the Morgan Wallens interested in our songs. Because, you know, that's where the money is."

They've agreed to get back together to finish the tune. Such is the life of the Nashville songwriter, striking up new artistic alliances almost daily.

"There are days when I don't know where I'm going or who I'm writing with until I look at my calendar," Irwin says.

The most successful Nashville songwriters, he adds, are those who are most likely to strike up positive relationships with fellow writers who have radically differing outlooks. For Irwin, that comes naturally.

"I'm easy to get along with, kind of a chameleon," he smiles. "Bartending skills, you know."

***

One of these days the expanding circumference of Nashville will swallow the bustling burg of Franklin, but not yet. For now, Main Street hums with private shops and restaurants, and the tallest thing in town, aside from a church steeple or two, is a slender monument topped by a Confederate soldier, standing at ease behind his rifle.

Outsiders might object to this sustained glorification of the Rebel cause, erected by the United Daughters of the Confederacy in 1899. ("Our heroes in gray shall ever live," the inscription reads.) But then again, from his high perch, that hero's eternal curse is to gaze directly down on a polished statue representing an advancing member of the United States Colored Troops. ("The Union Forever," his taunting inscription proclaims.) The Black trooper's back faces the Williamson County Courthouse steps, where men, women and children were sold into slavery at open markets.

Such is the complicated history of the steadily urbanizing South, which is banking its future financial strength in the attraction of talented people of all persuasions.

Franklin is about twenty miles south of Nashville—far enough away to escape the increasing big-town frenzy, close enough for an easy commute to the studios on Music Row. It's home to lots of country music performers like Keith Urban, Miley Cyrus, and Carrie Underwood.

A longtime member of the Nashville music community is Lisa Stewart, a singer and songwriter whose career has embraced gospel, country, blues, and Jazz. First a child church soloist, at age eleven she was performing country songs at a Nashville Fan Fair tent show—a gig that led to cutting her first record in the legendary music crucible of Muscle Shoals, Alabama. She signed her first country recording contract at age twenty-three and released three singles from her first album.

As a country artist, Stewart has performed around the world both as a solo act and backup singer—but now she's shifted gears to make her mark as a jazz singer, performing regularly with a combo that includes drummer Chester Thompson, who's played with Genesis and Frank Zappa's Mothers of Invention.

Needless to say, a diversified career like Stewart's has forced her into proximity with collaborators whose backgrounds and beliefs span a nearly limitless spectrum. But in each and every project, she tells me, all that really matters is the music.

Lisa Stewart (Michael Gomez Photography)

"I grew up listening to everything from B.B. King to David Bowie," Stewart tells me, sitting in the brightly lit living room of her home in Franklin. "In the church, we heard wonderful gospel music. My parents loved traditional country music, like Loretta Lynn and Conway Twitty. The radio in my brother's bedroom was blaring Led Zeppelin, Bowie, and The Rolling Stones."

As a result, Stewart found it difficult to assign different kinds of music to their own separate bins. She quotes the great jazzman Louis Armstrong: "All music is folk music. I ain't never heard a horse sing a song."

"And he's right," she says. "As humans, we want to categorize everything. But there's no real reason to. The very fact that there is such variety in music is what binds us together as musicians and music lovers."

And then Stewart repeats an observation I've heard from just about everyone I'm encountering in and around Nashville: Country music, in particular, is uniquely positioned among musical genres as a medium for affinity among people who would otherwise consider themselves to be fundamentally different.

"The great writers—Jimmy Rogers, Emmett Miller, Johnny Cash, Merle Haggard—they're all writing about things that people deal with on a daily basis, no matter what their background," she says. "They're writing about the working man. Tammy Wynette is singing songs about heartache. It's the real stuff that appeals to people from a very authentic place."

There's a saying in Nashville, Stewart tells me: *Clever is not cool.*

"Don't try to do anything but be authentic. You want to be real."

***

Music has long been Nashville's Great Equalizer. In the days after the Civil War, it was the music of Nashville that, for the very first time, brought white audiences—both in America's northern states and the world beyond—eye-to-eye with the newly freed Black people who, until then, had existed for them mostly as an abstraction.

It is November, 2021. And today, that mission of familiarization continues, spearheaded by the Nashville choral group that started it all more than 150 years ago: The Fisk Jubilee Singers of Fisk University.

The packed audience in Ryman Auditorium falls silent, eyes and ears focused on the very same proscenium stage where Ernest Tubb once went, "Walking the Floor Over You" and Jim Reeves whispered "He'll Have to Go." From the wings of that empty stage, the voices of nine young African American singers blend in a mesmerizing, almost whispering, rendition of the timeless slave spiritual, "Steal Away."

The singers wander into view, sojourners united in song. *The trumpet sounds within my soul*, they sing. *I ain't got long to stay here.*

Most often, it takes even a seasoned performer a song or two before they have an audience in their hands. But tonight, the Fisk Jubilee Singers have taken immediate hold of 2,000 hearts. If you're not wiping away tears, you are letting them flow, unashamed, down your cheeks.

Among the tearful is Dr. Paul Kwami, the group's musical director of twenty-eight years and child of Ghana, himself a former Fisk University student.

"It happens sometimes," he tells me several months after that concert marking the group's 150th anniversary. "I'm crying, the singers are crying. We're all crying."

We are seated in folding chairs, feeling warm sun pour through the windows of the Fisk Jubilee Singers' rehearsal room. It's the largest room in Jubilee Hall, a towered Victorian-era edifice at one end of the Fisk University campus. The school was founded in 1866, in those heady—but all-too-brief—days when hopes ran high that Reconstruction would bring a measure of equality to America's formerly enslaved people.

No one knew if there would be enough student interest to support such a school. Then, some 900 young students, virtually all of them recently emancipated, enrolled.

But while there was no shortage of students, money proved hard to come by. Strapped for cash, by 1871 the university was in danger of going under. The school's music professor and treasurer, George L. White, hit on a plan so crazy it just might work: He and Fisk's fledgling choir—four men and five women—would head out on a nationwide tour to raise money.

As it turned out, the general concept was sound: Audiences turned out to see and hear the singers. The execution, however, seemed weirdly dissonant: The choir members, all of them formerly enslaved young people, exclusively performed Western classical music. In other words, the songs of their enslavers. Everyone involved—chorus and audiences alike—seemed uncomfortable.

The final straw came during a church concert in Oberlin, Ohio. As the Fisk Singers performed from the balcony, the congregation basically stopped listening mid-concert. Worse, the singers could barely be heard as members of the supposed audience strolled from pew to pew, engaging in loud, rude conversation.

Telling this story, Kwami smiles broadly, his voice filling the choir's rehearsal space.

"Finally," he recounts, "one of the singers said, 'If they're not going to listen to us, then let's just sing for ourselves.' And they did. They started singing 'Steal Away.'"

The audience fell silent. They had never heard anything like this before.

"They thought Negro music was what they'd heard in minstrel shows," Kwami says. "The Negro spiritual was completely new to them."

Finally, the singers and their audiences had found a way to establish a two-way channel for their shared human experience. The Fisk Jubilee Singers, true to themselves at last, enthralled audiences throughout the East and Upper Midwest, roughly tracing the path of the pre-Civil War era Underground Railroad.

One noted writer—a man notoriously difficult to impress—was ecstatic.

"I do not know when anything has so moved me as did the Jubilee Singers," wrote Mark Twain, who'd grown up in the South hearing these same songs. "One must have been a slave himself in order to feel what that life was and so convey the pathos of it in the music."

During that first eighteen-month tour, the group raised about $40,000—the rough equivalent of $1 million today.

But success came at great cost to the original Jubilee singers: On the road for years saving for their school, the first nine never found time to earn their degrees. Only a few years ago were they given posthumous diplomas.

Among those selfless singers was Thomas Rutling. Born into slavery, he never knew his father, and his only memory of his mother, as a two-year-old, was of kissing her goodbye as she was taken away.

"Can you imagine someone living with that?" Kwami asks, shaking his head. "And yet he became a Fisk Jubilee singer who gave up his education, along with the others, to prevent the closure of this university."

Behind the stage of the Jubilee singers' rehearsal hall hangs a large painting that depicts eleven African American men and women in formal dress, posing in an ivy-draped colonnade. The group portrait was done in 1873, during the group's first European tour.

Following a royal command performance in London, Queen Victoria reportedly remarked, "You must come from a city of music!"

An exhibit at the Fisk Jubilee Singers exhibit in Nashville's nearby Musicians Hall of Fame suggests that Her Majesty's somewhat random comment was the genesis of Nashville's "Music City" nickname. But even the museum's archivist, Jay McDowell, takes that with a grain of salt.

"There's some doubt," he says, "but it's still a great story."

As the newspaperman says at the end of John Ford's *The Man Who Shot Liberty Valance*, "When the legend becomes fact, print the legend."

Legends, however, do die. Mere months after we met that sun-drenched day at Fisk University, just weeks before the choir's 151st anniversary, Dr. Paul Theophilus Kwami passed away suddenly. He was seventy.

***

It may be that the modern roots of Nashville's present-day collaborative renaissance stretch about forty miles south, just across the state border.

The recording studio known as 3614 North Jackson Highway in Muscle Shoals, Alabama, isn't much to look at, inside or out. Squat and square, the concrete block structure has all the charm of a coffin showroom — which, in fact, it was for twenty years before the guys with guitars showed up.

I'm starting to wonder if this place was worth the trip when my guide casually comments,

"...and this is the bathroom where Keith Richards finished writing 'Wild Horses.'"

That gets my attention.

We're standing at the open door of a tiny powder room just off this bare-bones recording studio. I peer inside. Clearly, there was only one place for the guitarist to sit while polishing The Rolling Stones' 1971 classic.

FAME Studios Music Booth

It's a weirdly surreal image, and so is that of Mick Jagger, Mick Taylor, Bill Wyman and Charlie Watts hanging around this studio, smoking and drinking and waiting for their comrade to emerge from the loo with the fruits of his bathroom inspiration.

They weren't alone. In fact, Muscle Shoals — a universe away from London, New York, and Motown — has for decades drawn a galaxy of recording legends of endless backgrounds, politics and persuasions. All found their way here to soak in the town's backwoods vibe.

From 3614 North Jackson Highway studio, I head about two miles north, to nearby Florence, where the Muscle Shoals music renaissance began. In the late 1950s, an enterprising local fiddler named Rick Hall opened FAME studios above a drug store. By 1963 he'd relocated to a small recording studio he built in Muscle Shoals.

I'm sitting in Rick Hall's cluttered office, up a narrow stairway from the modest FAME reception area, preserved in the exact condition it was when the Grammy-winning producer died in 2018. On the walls hang a gallery of gold records and photos of artists who stepped up to the microphones in the studio downstairs, a diverse crowd that includes Etta James, Wilson Pickett, The Osmonds, Little Richard, Paul Anka, Mac Davis, Duane Allman, Steven Tyler, and Aretha Franklin.

If that lineup sounds unexpectedly racially diverse for rural Alabama in the 1960s, that also explains the uncommon success of Rick Hall as a music producer: He didn't care what color a performer's skin was.

If he thought they could make a hit record, they were in.

And so, in these four walls, Etta James recorded her early hit, "Tell Mama." Wilson Pickett spun out with "Mustang Sally." The Osmonds found "One Bad Apple." Percy Sledge screamed, "When a Man Loves a Woman." Mac Davis pleaded, "Baby, Don't Get Hooked on Me." And Jerry Reed complained, "She Got the Goldmine/I Got the Shaft."

Muscle Shoals nurtured more than a recording environment — it was the birthplace of a unique sound, nurtured by Hall and embodied in a house band that fused funk, rock, and country into what became known as the Muscle Shoals Sound.

When Paul Simon decided to record tracks for his 1986 album *Graceland* at Muscle Shoals, he told his producer he wanted to get that great Black backup group he'd heard on so many Muscle Shoals albums.

We can only imagine his surprise to learn that "great Black backup group" was a bunch of white guys who'd grown up in the northern reaches of Alabama.

They called themselves The Swampers, and they were immortalized by Lynyrd Skynyrd, who gave them a shout-out in the group's iconic anthem, "Sweet Home Alabama," recorded in Muscle Shoals:

The sole surviving member of the Swampers is David Hood, bass player extraordinaire. We're sharing a table at the 360 Grille, a rotating restaurant high atop the Renaissance Shoals Resort and Spa in Florence. The sun is setting beyond the Tennessee River below, turning its course into a ribbon of red.

"The Muscle Shoals Sound is a lot of things and it's hard to describe," says Hood. "Funk was at the root of it, especially in the early years. The sound often combines rock, soul, funk and blues."

In 1969, after a long residency at FAME studios, the Swampers struck out to start their own recording company. Its official name was The Muscle Shoals Sound Studio, but that first year Cher recorded a solo album there. She called the album "3614 Jackson Highway," and that became the studio's unofficial title.

Touring 3614 North Jackson Highway, you can still see the corner where Hood sat playing his bass for the Staples Singers — creating what many still call the most distinctive bass line of all time for their song "I'll Take You There." In fact, if you listen carefully to the recording, you'll hear Mavis Staples say Hood's name three times, urging him on.

"I was thrilled," recalls Hood. "It was a magical session in so many ways. Mavis is still one of my favorite people."

A few feet away, you can peer in (but, as a sign warns, not use) that fateful powder room where Keith Richards found inspiration. The Rolling Stones were in Muscle Shoals just three days in early December 1969 — there's a historical sign at the site of the former Holiday Inn where they stayed — and in that time they laid down two of their most memorable hits: "Wild Horses" and "Brown Sugar."

***

From our table high above Muscle Shoals, David Hood is watching the red of the Tennessee River turn to deep purple, nearly fading into the shadows of the distinctive cliffs that line the opposite bank.

"A lot of people say the magic here is 'in the water,'" he says. "But we think it's much more than that. The studio musicians were a big attraction — and it was a small town without a lot of distractions. The artists could be more productive.

"And most important: It didn't matter who you were, or where you were from, or what kind of person you were. If you could make good music, you could make great music here."

***

Back in Nashville, the 5,021st live radio broadcast of The Grand Ole Opry is wrapping up at the Grand Ole Opry House, the institution's home since leaving Ryman Auditorium in 1974. In sharp contrast to the intimate confines of Ryman, the "new" place is a cavernous, Radio City Music Hall-class 4,000-seat auditorium. The two-hour show (including a fifteen-minute intermission) has been a heady mix of young'uns and old timers, including ninety-year-old Bobby Osborne, who seems as far removed from 2024 inductee Lainie Wilson as George Washington is from that granddaughter of yours who you think could be President someday.

For the finale, The Isaacs, recently installed as the newest members of the Opry, assemble onstage to bring down the curtain with an acapella rendition of the gospel standard (and unofficial national anthem of the Opry) "Will the Circle Be Unbroken." From my position in the wings, stage right, I can see what the performers see: A sea of phone-waving, enraptured humanity, as carried away as any Pentecostal congregation I've ever witnessed.

The song ends. The crowd roars. The announcer signs off. Another show in the can. The performers wave goodbye and half of them head my way. I step back to let them by.

Backstage at The Grand Ole Opry

Each one bears an ebullient smile, as if they can't believe their good fortune.

Gentle reader, I truly wish I could include in this examination of the things that connect Americans a chapter on the church. But looking back on that moment at the Grand Ole Opry, in March of 2022, I somberly realize that this musical benediction, a call to brotherhood across generations and cultures, is the closest I can come to that.

The Tennessee Eleven

Nashville, Tennessee: Taking Aim at Gun Violence

Finding a Crossfire Approach

Earlier, I suggested that abortion may be the nation's most divisive issue. But I don't think I'd get a serious argument for saying that guns are a strong number two (with a bullet, I'd say, if I had an affinity for bad puns).

Similarly, at the outset of this journey I pretty much despaired of finding anyone making headway trying to reconcile two sides that hold, with equal passion, the position that they are the ones interested in preserving lives and safety.

So imagine my relief to learn that our old friends at Builders Movement—the same folks who somehow fostered a dialogue between sides in the abortion debate—had done much the same thing regarding guns.

And in the staunchly firearms-friendly state of Tennessee, no less.

Jaila Hampton and Jay Zimmerman each arrived at their feelings about guns honestly.

Jay grew up in northeastern Tennessee, hunting with his grandfather just to put food on the table.

"I was more excited about getting my first shotgun than I was about learning how to drive or getting my first girlfriend," he says. "Where I come from, firearms are absolutely a part of the culture; part of the heritage that is passed down from generation to generation."

A seven-year overseas military stint deployed as a parachutist, combined with his current career as a mental health worker specializing in suicide prevention, have shaded his childhood enthusiasm.

"Hunting isn't as important to me as it used to be," he admits. "War changes your outlook on taking the life of another living thing. But it has not affected my relationship with firearms. I still enjoy shooting: the physics of pulling the trigger and the explosion of a shell in your hand and the whole idea of a round going downrange and hitting a target.

"That love was instilled in me by my grandfather, and I still have it."

Jaila, now a college freshman, grew up in Memphis, a town that has long had a checkered history with firearms: In 2023 alone, 399 people died of gunshot wounds in the medium-sized city. Still, until she was sixteen, Jaila somehow managed to remain untouched by gun violence.

Then came August, 2021. In broad daylight on a hot summer afternoon, Jaila's best friend, seventeen-year-old Braylon Murray, was gunned down outside a Memphis car wash.

"My heart actually hurt," she says now. "There was this physical pain; this emptiness. I kept thinking of our last conversation: He'd had a friend that was killed. He said he was tired of losing people. He was upset by the state of our city, and where it was going."

Cruelly, Jaila's initial first-hand experience with fatal gun violence was just the beginning.

"After that," she says with a shiver, "it was like dominoes. Kids were dropping like flies."

Her eyes open wide, in continuing disbelief.

"I know people who lost their entire high school friend group. They were, literally, the only ones left standing."

She shakes her head.

"That's not normal. I guess there's a part of life where you'd expect the people you know to start passing away. When you're old, maybe. But not when you're sixteen."

There has to be a way, she insists, to head off gun violence. And at least part of that solution, Jaila believes, has to be some control over who gets to hold a firearm in their hand.

"I grew up loving Memphis," she says. "And I just want to see it better, and safer, for kids like myself."

***

Jaila Hampton

I first encountered Jay and Jaila in a documentary, *The Tennessee 11*, chronicling a group of people with diverse opinions on gun policy who, through a multi-day process of airing their differences and discovering their common goals, hammered out a list of legislative proposals for presentation to the state legislature.

Gathered by Builders Movement, this group convened in the wake of one of Tennessee's darkest hours: the March 27, 2023 mass shooting at The Covenant School, a private Christian academy in Nashville's Green Hills neighborhood. Three nine-year-olds and three adults were murdered by twenty-eight-year-old Aiden Hale, who was in turn killed by Metropolitan Police.

Hale had stormed the school wielding an AR-pistol, a 9 mm carbine rifle, and a hand gun.

For a moment there, the Covenant School Shooting seemed to be a flex point for Nashville, and for Tennessee, on the subject of gun violence. Yes, there was the usual outpouring of sympathy: flowers at the school grounds, "thoughts and prayers" from politicians, GoFundMe pages to help grieving families cope with funeral expenses.

In the Tennessee State Capitol, three liberal representatives led observers seated in the public gallery, chanting, "We have to do better" and "Gun reform now." (Two legislators were expelled; both were reinstated by their constituents a week later.)

Jay Zimmerman

In a bipartisan measure, the legislature quickly passed laws funding the presence of armed School Resource Officers (SROs) on every school campus in the state.

The measure was met with scorn as too little, too late from many members of the public, leading Governor Bill Lee to call an August special session of the General Assembly to focus on gun violence and what—if anything—to do about it. Lee, who had lost two people he knew in the shooting, listed his modest priorities, most of which were only tangentially related to guns, including funding for mental illness programs, DNA collection at the time of felony arrests, a new study on human trafficking, the elimination of taxes on firearm safes and safety devices, and free gun locks for firearm owners.

At the same time the special session was meeting, a few miles away, the eleven-member Builders Movement panel met in a Nashville conference center for a multi-day "Solution Session." As is the model for most groups of this sort, the first day or so was spent simply getting to know each other, fostering the notion that, despite what the media might try to tell you, even those who hold positions diametrically opposed to yours are fully and reassuringly human.

(On the first day of Tennessee's special legislative session, gun rights advocates adopted a rule allowing them to turn off the microphone of any speaker they wanted.)

The Builders Movement's getting-to-know-you process is crystalized in the opening minutes of the Tennessee 11 documentary as the participants, besides Jalia Hampton and Jay Zimmerman, introduce themselves:

Tim Carroll is a firearms instructor ("Gun policy and gun safety…those are key words for anyone who's a Second Amendment advocate"). Alyssa Pearman is a high school English teacher who lost two students in shootings ("It's just seems to keep happening, and it has to stop"). Brandi Kellett is a college professor who knows a child who survived the Covenant Shooting ("I don't see our legislature moving on this issue. I feel stuck"). Pastor William Green's mother was terrorized by an armed home invader ("It nudged me toward the Second Amendment"). Arriel Gipson Martin works for the Memphis City government and owns several guns ("I think we have a lot of unhealed trauma in our communities"). Adam Luke is a mental health professional who grew up hunting, but sees the effects of trauma in his practice ("I'm actually excited for this conversation because I think we can come out with something"). Ron Johnson is director of safety in the Nashville Mayor's Office ("I grew up in North Memphis, in the projects…if I didn't play sports I would probably be in prison or dead. That's where most of my friends are"). Pastor Kevin Shrum writes pro-Second Amendment op-eds in local newspapers ("I wrote an article that I titled 'People Kill People'…We've got some work to do in our cultural institutions, which seem to be fracturing"). Recently retired Tennessee Highway Patrol Captain Mark Proctor is still haunted by images of gun violence ("I've had weapons pulled on me; pulled (weapons) on people in order to get them to comply…I feel like I can bring a lot to the table").

Hearing these thumbnail autobiographies, it's clear to me that Builders has been scrupulous in not stacking the deck regarding one position or another. I notice almost immediately, those involved seem considerably less strident than the folks we're used to seeing delivering pro- or anti-gun talking points on TV.

I mention this to Ashley Phillips, the head of programs for Builders Movement. She seems happy that I noticed.

"It's important to recruit people who are willing to have a real, substantive conversation about guns," she says, sitting at her home office desk in Boston. "We're not looking for policy wonks. They don't need to be experts, but they do need to have some level of technical or lived experience that would enable them to have those productive conversations."

Before launching a discussion group in a state, Builders sends an advance team to recruit possible members.

"We try to bring in people who are representative of a state's population," she continues. "It's not a perfect ratio, but we do seek out people who are passionate about an issue and who also have knowledge about it. There are other, intangible qualities: Are they willing to listen? Are they humble? Are they going to learn from others? Are they there for the goal of problem solving? It's kind of a puzzle to get the right mix."

(Early in the special Tennessee legislative session, lawmakers passed a rule banning observers from holding signs as large as a standard sheet of paper.)

To me, the big surprise—considering how we're all being beaten over the head with reports of American polarization—is how readily Builders can apparently find fair-minded participants. My discovery, I learn from Ashley, feeds right into the optimism inherent in Builders' model.

"We find that most Americans want to find common ground," she says. "They want to be generous towards one another, even if we don't see that generous attitude or pursuit of common ground playing out in the media or in social media."

Most importantly, she adds, Builders' Solution Session facilitators never pressure anyone to compromise their basic values and convictions.

"The thing is," she says, "there's enough common ground that they can sort of just set aside the places where they don't agree."

(After one Republican Tennessee House member accused hardline gun legislators of being like ostriches with their heads in the sand, a senator posted a photo of an ostrich egg on X and sneered, "It must be egghausting sending so many bills…instead of doing the work the people sent us here to do.")

Jaila Hampton, the panel member who lost a childhood friend to gun violence, and Jay Zimmerman, the veteran who's been a gun enthusiast since childhood, live at opposite ends of the state, so we are meeting up on a computer screen. As Jay describes his initial impressions upon entering the conference center meeting room, it becomes immediately clear why he was a perfect choice to participate.

"I'm always open to civil discourse and discussion," he tells me. "I love to learn, and I don't think you can learn if you're not willing to listen.

"The fact is, I suspect my perspective on guns is unique to me—just like everyone sitting at that table has unique perspectives of their own."

Looking back on that first session, Jaila recalls no sense of worry over coming face-to-face with people who held opinions that ran counter to hers.

"Maybe I wasn't worried enough!" she laughs. "I mean, here were eleven people in a room, all of them with different perspectives.

"But I've grown up doing community leadership programs, learning about diverse life experiences, and how to have healthy conversations about them."

Adds Jay, "I come from a family that has divisions of its own. So, I kind of went into the week thinking, 'Well, this may turn out to be like spending Thanksgiving with my cousins!'"

(On day three of the special Tennessee legislative session, lawmakers ejected from a hearing the mother of a child murdered in the Covenant School shooting, along with several other people who were accused of holding paper signs.)

***

Possibly drawing from Thanksgiving experiences of their own, the Tennessee 11 had no expectations of finding common ground on the broad issues that divide the country on guns: Outlawing certain types of weapons, limiting amounts of gun ownership, setting age limits on gun ownership, to name a few.

But as the days progressed, the panel found a growing level of agreement when it came to the necessity for carefully drawn regulations under which someone may not be sold a gun, or else have their weapon removed from them, if only temporarily.

As so often happens when people of differing perspectives begin discussing a sticky issue, the matter of definitions provided the initial obstacle.

"The people strongly on the side of the Second Amendment at first bristled at the mention of what are commonly called Red Flag laws," Ashley recalls. "They said, 'There's no way I can support that.' So, we suggested they put aside the label of 'Red Flag' and their own preconceived notions about what that meant."

Sidestepping the label, the group considered the hypothetical case of someone who is actively making threats against someone, or displaying erratic behavior toward themselves or others.

"Well, everyone agreed that person should not have a gun in their possession, at least not until this episode has passed," says Ashley.

But while the less gun-friendly side of the panel would have enacted a swift and decisive gun confiscation procedure, the Second Amendment supporters feared the process could easily be misused to enact wholesale weapon removal.

"The discussion turned to looking at things like, 'What structures are in place to make sure that the process is fair?'" Ashley recalls. "And how do we guarantee that the gun owner gets his or her firearm back once they've emerged from that troubled emotional state?

"Having that nuanced conversation, and having the space to really spread out and talk about the issue in the context of somebody's life in a real situation, allowed the group to find unexpected, hidden common ground."

And it all became possible only after dispatching with the generic label "Red Flag," which itself had coincidentally become one.

"It's so interesting," says Ashley, "it wasn't even on our agenda, but they all got to talking about the importance of language and words, and the ways we choose to talk about policy: What one person might define in a certain way versus the way somebody else might define it."

Huddling in conversation, the group created a white board display they called "The Wall of Words." *How, they asked each other, do you define "Red Flag Law?" How do you define "Assault Weapon?" What does it mean to you? Here's what it means to me. How should we agree to define it?*

"The goal," says Ashley, "was to come up with common language that would enable them to have productive conversations—not making assumptions about what people mean by certain words."

The Wall of Words—and the subsequent realization that mutual understanding can be foiled by something as innocuous as vocabulary—provided an important step in the group's journey, helping cement their identity as people with differing viewpoints but shared priorities.

"When we left, many of us were still on the complete opposite ends of the spectrum when it came to firearms and ownership," says Jay. "But we all decided to reject the perspective of all those people who want to focus on the things we disagree on."

Primarily, Jay objected to the tendency in America to villainize people over politics.

"Why do I need to say, 'If I don't agree with you, I can't like you as a person'?" he asks.

"Let's focus on the eighty percent that we agree on, rather than on the twenty percent we don't. And, yes, let's keep having conversations about that twenty percent.

"Jaila and me, we probably don't agree on firearms. But I think she's a great person."

Jaila smiles.

"Everybody has to be willing to take part in tough conversations," she says. "But you also have to remain kind, and understand that everybody's perspectives are valid."

As would clearly be the case from the start, Tennessee's special legislative session was gaveled to a close in what the New York Times termed "chaos." The session, called to reassure residents of Tennessee that their legislators were serious about protecting their children from gun violence, managed to pass one gun-related measure: Funding for a firearm safety ad campaign.

Meanwhile, once they got their vocabulary issues sorted out, the Tennessee 11—ordinary citizens who represented a wide range of positions regarding gun rights and ownership—framed five concrete proposals taking aim at gun violence in Tennessee, explaining in their summary that "Every American has a right to safety and also a right to own guns, valued by some as a way to ensure their safety."

Their proposals:

1) **Develop and promote tools for responsible gun ownership.** Including: A tool for federally licensed firearms sellers, private sellers, and trainers to assess, intervene, and flag people who are seeking to own or use firearms illegally. A toolkit to support someone holding a gun securely for a struggling friend or family member. A voluntary background check system.

2) **Develop gun issue literacy resources for schools, communities, and media.** School resources could be integrated into existing social emotional learning, health, or civics curriculums. Media resources could include an unbiased language guide that defines factual terminology to discuss gun issues. Training community leaders on existing laws, safe gun use, safe storge and de-escalation tips.

3) **Reduce trauma that contributes to gun violence by investing in communities.** To reduce gun violence, society and the state must reduce Adverse Childhood Experiences (ACEs) and adult trauma. Approaches might include early childhood education investments, family engagement, school & community-based services, culturally tailored mental health services, and increased economic opportunity for impacted neighborhoods.

4) **Broaden the School Resource Officer role to include law enforcement and human services.** In addition to law enforcement training, SROs (sworn law enforcement officers with arrest powers working in schools) should hone human services practices grounded in restorative justice, which views justice as "repair" of the harm vs. "punishment" for it.

5) **Allow temporarily removal of firearms based on risk of violence.** Risk of violence should be the primary criteria for removal, since mental illness is not a good predictor of who will commit interpersonal violence...Criteria for removal should include history of violence, erratic behavior, making threats, stalking, sharing plans or desires to hurt oneself or others, or other behavior that is a strong indicator of violence. There should also be clear and reasonable criteria for how an individual can get their firearm back.

Once the five suggestions were agreed upon, Builders invited all residents of Tennessee to weigh in online, voting "Agree," "Disagree," or "Undecided." Solid majorities of fifty-eight to sixty-five percent agreed with the first four; the temporary firearm removal proposal squeaked by in the approval column at fifty-one percent.

Considering the realities of Tennessee politics, the group decided their best chance at helping form state policy would be to unite behind a single plank from their final platform: The guns literacy program for public schools. In 2024, a bill closely resembling The Tennessee 11's proposal passed the State Legislature and was signed into law.

"It's an interesting juxtaposition, isn't it?" asks Builders' Ashley Phillips. "Here we have eleven citizens, who would normally never be sitting face to face, tackling an issue that their lawmakers are also tackling just a few miles down the road, both in response to this tragic event that had happened in their community a few months prior. The lawmakers go through a chaotic special session and don't come up with anything. But the citizens, well, they walk away with actual proposals, hammered out despite their disagreements. That just wows me. It goes to show that when it comes down to it, citizens do agree on a lot of things. And they want their representatives to come together to solve problems."

It also goes to show: People don't kill good policy. Politicians do.

Matt & Jackie Maryak

Asheville, North Carolina: After the Storm

You Need an (R) and a (D) to spell "Rescued"

The story of my sister-in-law Jackie and her husband Matt and the hurricane from Hell and the disappearing mountainside and the armed men in battle fatigues who appeared out of nowhere to bring them free satellite hookups so they could tell their families they were still alive is going to take some telling, but please…trust me that it will eventually circle back to what this book is about.

For now, let's just jump to the double-pronged moral: You can be a red state right-wing paramilitary operative and still have a heart for your political opposite. And even a couple of classic center-left liberals who've spent the past few decades living a stone's throw from Augusta National Golf Club can become friends for life with a man who emerges from the woods with a gun.

There. Now let's back up a bit.

Gather 'round, children, for what my family has come to refer to as *Jackie and Matt's Great Adventure*—a story that, having unfolded just a few weeks before my encounter with the Man in the Red Cap, became the foundation for the book you hold in your hands.

***

You may recall a hurricane called Helene, a tropical behemoth that dumped bathtubs of rain on western North Carolina, causing catastrophic flooding and untold mayhem across the area in late September 2024. As I write this, at a time when Helene is just about all anyone is talking about, it seems ludicrous to add a memory jogger regarding the storm. But while everyone right now is saying, "We'll never forget Helene," history tells us in six months we'll also be vowing to never forget Norman or Tony or Zacchaeus, or whatever names will be attached to subsequent Storms of the Century.

For most of us, Helene would soon become "The really bad hurricane down south that washed all those towns away." But for the tens of thousands of people who happened to live in Helene's path – clinging to trees and boulders while their homes, transformed into perversely personal Noah's Arks, floated down brown-water-choked hollers and river valleys – Helene became an historic inflection point rivaling, and perhaps surpassing, Pearl Harbor and 9/11.

My brother-in-law Matt Maryak is a retired nuclear power engineer and Jackie, sister of my wife Carolyn, is winding down her career securing credentials for health professionals. It's a job Jackie can easily tackle remotely from the couple's perch in a strikingly beautiful wooden chalet halfway up a mountain in the town of Swannanoa, northeast of Asheville.

In recent decades, Asheville, a former mining and lumber town, has ranked among the trendiest retirement communities in the country. Of course, one main difference between retiring to the mountains of North Carolina and, say, The Villages in Florida is that they don't make a golf cart that will carry you up a mile-long, six percent-grade gravel road—which is the only way to get to Matt and Jackie's home.

From afar, it has long seemed to me that folks retire to The Villages – or the Delaware Beaches, where I live – largely to become part of a vital community with stores and restaurants virtually around the block. Conversely, residents of the Asheville exurbs are more content to sit by themselves on their treetop-level decks and glory in the sunset, listening to country music while drinking volumes of liquor they'd never dream of consuming if they had to drive home. And if they do want to motor into town to pick up some food, eat at one of America's best restaurants or sit in on the Friday night drum circle, then that's all just a half-hour drive away in downtown Asheville.

All of that has everything to do with why, a few years ago, Jackie and Matt sold their longtime home in Augusta, Georgia, and moved up here full-time.

When Helene crashed into the Florida Panhandle, 370 miles south of Asheville, on September 26, 2024, the experienced mountain folk braced themselves, but only moderately, with a sense of calm familiarity. Despite the undeniable hydrological reality that rain falling on mountains funnels itself through valleys with exponentially increasing levels of violence, almost no one was expecting the storm to open Hell's floodgates. This is why Jackie and Matt did not hightail it out of there. And neither did their neighbors, scattered in some forty or so homes, ranging from rustic to luxurious, up and down their shared mountainside. Over the years they'd all ridden out raging onslaughts of rain, snow, and hail. As Helene approached, most felt they were fully prepared to deal with the attendant power outages and temporary isolation that would inevitably result as nearby Bee Tree Creek spilled over the concrete bridge that linked them to Bee Tree Road, what passes for a throughfare in these parts.

Few thought that Helene would do the kind of damage that could not be overcome with a chain saw and a 4x4 pickup truck. Typically, there was little, if any, before-the-fact planning among the neighbors, who, in the best mountain man-and-woman tradition, pretty much kept to themselves.

"We have a friend who works at the Biltmore in Asheville," says Matt. "They have a meteorologist on staff, and every day, as the storm intensified, she would forward us his twice-daily formal weather reports.

"By Thursday, the day the storm hit, it had already been raining for days. And now they were saying this could be a 1,000-year storm. Loss of life. Devastation."

As we discuss Helene and its aftermath, Jackie, Matt and I are at a family Thanksgiving gathering in Pittsburgh, hundreds of miles away from the scene. Still, it is barely two months since the hurricane came heaving down their holler, and at times as they relive the ordeal, I can sense an occasional crack of PTSD-like desperation in their voices.

As the storm intensified Thursday afternoon, Jackie and Matt drove two of their cars down the mountainside, crossed the creek, and parked one of them about five miles from their home, on high ground in a church parking lot.

"Should we leave a note on the dashboard?" Jackie asked Matt, concerned about leaving the vehicle at a church they had never attended.

"Jackie," Matt answered, "if the weather forecast is right, nobody is going to give a shit about a car parked in their lot."

With that, the pair drove back across the creek and up the mountainside, then hunkered down in their home. Jackie sent one more text to her three sisters:

Ferocious storm since wee hours here with no end in sight. A small tree came down in our front but no damage. Power out since midnight, generator faulted out but Matt was somehow able to get it on. Thank god since it powers our well pump and everything. Eager to see our bridge and road.

And just like in a bad movie, as reports of devastation began filtering out of Asheville, that was the last we heard from them. Jackie and Matt's cell phone and Internet service, always dicey at best up here, was blown away by the hurricane's weakening, but still furious, winds.

***

Come daybreak, they had never seen anything remotely like what Nature had whipped up.

"It was just fierce outside," says Jackie. "Different from any other storm. The water, it was just flying down the mountain, like raging waterfalls, all around our house."

"There was this constant roaring sound that I assumed was the wind," Matt adds. "I went outside, and it wasn't the wind. It was the roar of the waterfalls. The raging sound of water pouring down the mountain."

Miraculously, the torrents somehow traced courses that diverged above Jackie and Matt's house and passed on either side, like a parting curtain.

When their house seems to be playing Red Sea in a Passover Pageant, you might expect the owners to stay put. And that's what Jackie and Matt would have done had Jackie not promised to look after a neighbor's kittens.

"Well, he asked me," Jackie says as Matt rolls his eyes at the memory. "He didn't know the world was going to end while he was out of town. So, we put on our waders and headed out."

Again, we are not talking here about a neighborhood like Mayfield, where June Cleaver straightens her pearls before heading next door to check on Lumpy Rutherford's pets. This is a close-to-vertical conglomeration of alpine homes built with the express intent of remaining, now and forever, out of sight of other alpine homes.

So, there were Jackie and Matt slogging through a diagonal river of muddy water, following as close as they could the path of the privately maintained loop road that connects the widely separated mountainside properties.

And then the road disappeared.

"The whole side of the mountain had pulled away," Jackie says with a shudder. "To our left, we could see a big crater where the land and trees used to be—and now the contents of that crater were piled on top of our road."

From here, Jackie and Matt could see to the cat owner's house. A food truck he'd been renovating was now, well, pretty much beyond renovation, having been tumbled and twisted by the avalanche.

Still, they managed to get to the house and tend to the kittens, who didn't even show any appreciation because, you know, cats.

"Oh, my God, so much shit," Jackie says, wide-eyed at the memory. "I had no idea kittens could shit so much."

The storm had passed by late Friday. Jackie and Matt just stewed in their house—strategically switching their generator on and off to save fuel, since no one had the vaguest idea when they'd be getting out of there.

Jackie's concern regarding her family's worries was, of course, well-founded. For days, just about the only word out of Swannanoa came via the news, and it was never good: Unhelpfully, one *Washington Post* headline proclaimed that Swannanoa had been "completely and entirely erased." Not just "entirely," but "completely *and* entirely."

***

Aside from the shifting physical landscape, something else had changed on Jackie and Matt's mountainside: The residents, who in normal times prided themselves on their self-reliance, began turning up at doors, checking on each other; offering help and emotional support. Those with generators brought refrigerated food to virtual strangers, and let people they hardly knew come in and recharge their devices. From top to bottom, the mountainside echoed with the sound of chain saws as neighbors helped neighbors free themselves from the death grip of fallen oak and hemlock trees.

Jackie and Matt's house became the central meeting point for updates and planning. Twice a day—at 10 a.m. and 4 p.m.—the group gathered around one neighbor's transistor radio to hear official updates.

Another neighbor, it so happened, subscribed to a particularly resilient cellular service that, days after the storm, finally offered a weak signal if you stood in the right place. They offered to let everyone make a call to the outside world. Jackie and Matt had a brief conversation with their two grown sons, who shared their relief with the extended family.

Still, that immovable landslide cut off an entire side of the mountaintop community, creating a dangerous barrier for those trying to move about the neighborhood, and clearly, the day-to-day power and hand tools owned by the mountain folk were not up to clearing the tons of landslide debris. Using their fragile cellular link, Jackie managed to call Carolyn with a request that she find some way to post on social media the news that there was an impassable landslide on a mountainside outside Asheville. (Carolyn, probably by virtue of being the youngest of four sisters, is somehow considered the most Internet-savvy member of the family. If anyone could figure out how to post a message on Facebook, all agreed, Carolyn would be the most likely one among them.)

Wielding her unique online genius, Carolyn did, indeed, find a Friends of Swannanoa page on Facebook, where, like the Electronic Age Wizardess that she is, she dutifully posted about Jackie and Matt and the Loop People, and asked if, maybe, someone could lend them a hand.

And that's where the guys with the guns come in.

***

Within minutes of Carolyn's Facebook post, around 6 p.m., Jackie's cell phone, now receiving weak signals, rang. It was a man who said he was with a volunteer group called Aerial Recovery.

What followed was, in Jackie's telling, one of those phone calls you see depicted in the movies, where a clip-voiced military officer commands a complex invasion on several fronts, barking orders and taking names.

"We've got a big team here," he said. "Been here since Day One. Love to help you with your landslide. We're coming up."

Now, you must understand that Jackie is the classic "I don't want to be a bother" kind of person, and at this point she was on the verge of telling this nice man not to make such a fuss.

"It's really treacherous," she protested. "The dirt road is just falling away. And I'm sure there are people who need Starlink more than we do…"

"Miss Jackie," the caller interrupted. "You have no idea—NO IDEA—the kinds of places we've dropped into. We are dropped into disasters of all kinds, all over the world. This is what we do."

Click.

As the sun set that night, Jackie and Matt wondered if they would ever see a hair of the guys from Aerial Recovery. And, if so, who in the world were they?

***

It was after dark that Matt heard his dog barking in that "strangers-a-comin" manner—a sound it had not made in days.

And then, like a pair of Rambos emerging from deep forest camouflage, there they were: Two muscular men in camo fatigues, tattoos disappearing up the sleeves of their aviator jackets, packing holstered pistols.

"Special Ops," Matt muttered to himself. "*What have we done*?"

Recalling that moment, Matt leans forward in his chair.

"You gotta understand," he says, eyes piercing mine. "We are out there in the middle of fucking *nowhere*. We're contacting random people we don't know on the Internet. And here are these two guys packing pistols on their hips."

Jackie nods solemnly.

"We were very, very vulnerable," she says.

As if to reassure the couple that this was strictly a business call, the men immediately asked Jackie and Matt to direct them to the landslide in question.

"Okay," said one of them, assessing the damage. "I know what we need. We'll be back tomorrow."

Before hiking back down the hill, the guys left them with a Starlink device that would enable them to hook up with one of Elon Musk's communications satellites.

"How do I get this back to you?" Jackie asked.

"Keep it," said one of them. "It's yours. The whole neighborhood can use it as a hub."

And then they were gone.

The next day, a whole team of workers showed up with turbocharged power tools that would make Paul Bunyan proud. Before the day was out, the landslide was cleared. Heading back up to Jackie and Matt's place, one of them noticed Matt struggling to cut through the trunk of a tree that had fallen above the house.

"It was ridiculous," Matt recalls. "I wasn't getting anywhere. All of a sudden, here's this Green Beret beside me, helping me cut this tree."

Matt thanked the guy profusely—and in response got a polite shake of the head.

"Thank *you*," the Green Beret said. "You're helping me get through this."

Which is a curious thing for a rescuer to say, until you understand what Aerial Recovery is all about.

***

Jay Carter

At this point I'm going to turn the narrative over to a fellow named Jay Carter, a longtime volunteer with Aerial Recovery. He's one of the two guys who, as they emerged from the forest, a) offered much-needed support to Jackie and Matt and b) caused Jackie and Matt to fear they might be reliving the opening scene of *Red Dawn*.

It is worth noting that Jay, after years of experience in the field, fully understands how intimidating he and his colleagues can appear to people who are already in the throes of life-altering chaos.

"A lot of people, you can see it in their faces," he tells me. "They're thinking, 'Holy cow—who are these big, jacked-up dudes?'

"But we are very, very careful in our approach to every situation. We make sure to tell them, before we ever walk up to them, that hey, we're here to help you.'"

That was the approach Jay and his partner took toward the visibly startled Jackie and Matt.

"We didn't mean to alarm you," Jay had told them calmly, keeping both is hands clearly in view. "Can we help you in any way?"

Jay Carter & Jackie Maryak

Almost imperceptibly, the rescuers had stepped closer to the couple speaking soothing words until they could sense the pair's growing comfort with the situation. As Jay described the process, I couldn't help but think of a cowboy trying to soothe a wild horse.

"We always have to remember," says Jay, "that this is just a Tuesday to us. But for them, it's the worst day of their lives."

Besides the immediate concern for their own physical safety, Jay says, lots of people in Jackie and Matt's situation are also leery of being victimized by one of those widely reported hucksters who are always trying to take advantage of disaster victims.

"They've heard about those guys who show up after a storm, say they're going to help—collect $10,000 and disappear," he says.

"The first thing we need to do is assure people that we're not asking for anything from them. All we want is the opportunity to help."

It's that concept of service as a privilege that defines Aerial Recovery. The nonprofit group hasn't been around long—just since 2020, when Britnie Turner, an anti-child trafficking activist, and her husband Jeremy Locke, a twenty-year U.S. Army Special Forces veteran, launched the program with two expressed aims: To provide essential assistance to disaster victims worldwide...and also to offer military veterans, who may have lost their sense of purpose, a chance to put their skills and instincts to work helping others.

As a veteran, Locke was painfully aware that many longtime military vets become overwhelmed with a sense of uselessness upon their discharge. In his case, leaving behind a career of leading life-saving missions left him feeling his best years were behind him and he began to sink into depression. With the creation of Aerial Recovery, Locke and Turner saw a chance to create a two-way dynamic, with veterans offering their lifesaving expertise while drawing from those they rescued the reassurance that they were, indeed, still needed.

Since then, the men and women of Aerial Recovery have been dispatched to offer aid in the wake of hurricanes, floods, fires, earthquakes and structural collapses. Volunteers also embark on highly dangerous missions to rescue victims of human trafficking.

But no one heads into the field with Aerial Recovery without first undergoing an intensive training regimen on the group's private island, located in the British Virgin Islands. Besides sharpening their rescue skills, the military veterans also bond as platoons, frankly discussing with each other the darker corners of their lives and mental states.

This psychological phase of training is essential: Early on, the founders learned that because many disaster scenes closely resemble the field of battle—and because the group often deploys to war-torn regions like Ukraine—military veterans may suffer debilitating PTSD flashbacks in the field.

The program isn't about fixing something broken, the group's website states, but rather "repurposing the skills, strength, and heart that these heroes had to offer."

***

Jay figures he's been on Aerial Recovery missions in seventeen states, plus several international trips. Unlike most members, he's not former military: He was a full-time firefighter in Valdosta, Georgia and also worked with Georgia's Search and Rescue Task Force 2.

"That involved really rigorous training," he recalls. "But I knew that was where I wanted to be. I wanted to change people's lives; to save people's lives. And I also wanted to show that there are people out there that care; people who are willing to do anything they can to help folks they don't even know."

Still, Jay found that working within the constraints of government could be frustrating. State and Federal rescue coordinators mean well, he says, but they are bound by rules and regulations that he feels can get in the way of conducting a successful rescue.

"Sometimes, government field units aren't allowed to make the call themselves as to whether they can go in on a rescue mission and make the grab or not," he says. "The call is made based on what computer technology is telling them regarding wind speeds, or temperatures, or other conditions—rather than on the observations of someone like me, who's actually standing in the field and is seeing the conditions first-hand."

Under Aerial Recovery's model, he says, the rescuer on the scene has the final say regarding a go-ahead order.

"Now I'm the guy that makes that call," he says. "I get to calculate when there's a 72-mph wind, or I'm standing in a flood, with my boots in the mud, whether or not I'm at risk—and when, maybe, I can push that risk a little more."

Because of that pushing-the-envelope model, Aerial Recovery rescuers often find themselves on the scene of a disaster before government units move in. The response isn't always immediately positive.

"The government guys have had experience with a lot of private organizations that like to cowboy up when a disaster strikes, but then they don't necessarily know what they're doing," Jay explains. "They have great hearts, and I respect them, but they don't have the training they need. They can get themselves hurt, which pulls the government guys away from rescuing someone else.

"Once the government guys realize we're a highly trained unit, and that we know what we're doing, we generally get a good response."

***

Given the fact that Aerial Recovery is populated primarily by ex-military people, it would come as no surprise that its membership skews heavily conservative. (A 2020 Pew Research Center study showed that less than twenty-six percent of all active military people identify as "Liberal".) But perhaps because America's military are conditioned to believe they protect all their countrymen, regardless of political stance, there seems to be nothing that matters less to Aerial Recovery members than who a disaster victim voted for.

"I look at it this way," says Jay. "Jesus Christ was a servant. And He was a servant to everybody. He didn't ask questions first.

"So, when we can come in and help people, when I can be the hands and feet of God in a bad situation, that's something to appreciate. I'm not just mouthing words when I thank someone for calling us in. I genuinely, honestly appreciate them allowing us to come in at the worst moment of their lives; to be here for them.

"I mean, what have words ever achieved? Action answers everything."

***

Aerial Recovery spent months, on and off, in Western North Carolina, delivering ten planes and numerous trucks loaded with supplies including food, water, propane, and medical kits. Each day they dispatched at least seven teams via land transport or helicopter to clear debris, repair roads, and remove trees from homes.

But the outpouring of generosity was not one-way: Across the region, churches, civic groups and individuals—representing a wide spectrum of social and political orientations—poured resources into Aerial Recovery's continuing efforts.

Looking back from the vantage point of Thanksgiving, Jackie recalls, "I finally just came out and insisted to Jay, 'Hey, what do you need the most?'"

Jay resisted the notion of accepting charity, but finally gave in (that's Jackie at work).

"Well," he said, "with winter coming, people who've been displaced by the storm and have nothing will be needing buddy heaters and propane to run them, because many of them are in damaged houses with no electricity, or worse – in tents or in the woods."

You probably don't know my sister-in-law Jackie, but if you did, you'd know that was absolutely all she needed to hear in order to mount a buddy heater quest that would rival the logistics of D-Day.

Immediately, her mind went to Chris and Retha, a British couple who'd been honeymooning in the vicinity and managed to get off the mountain a week or so after the storm. Jackie happened to know they were soon heading back to Swannanoa from Roanoke, Virginia, in a rental car to retrieve the van they had to leave behind because of that landslide.

Matt closes his eyes, smiles, and shakes his head.

"So, of course, Jackie calls the Home Depot in Roanoke to see if they have buddy heaters," he says. "And she talks to the manager, gets herself a discount, and then spends $3,000 to buy every one they've got. Plus, the little propane tanks."

Jackie jumps in: "So, I called Chris and Retha and said I needed them to pick all that stuff up, stick it into their rental car and then meet us in Swannanoa."

Now, Chris and Retha had already been on a BBC news program during the past week, telling the entire British Commonwealth about the amazing survival experience they'd had with their new American friends Jackie and Matt. So they were only too happy to help.

Matt met Chris and Retha, as agreed, in a Swannanoa parking lot to move the heaters and propane tanks from their rental car to his pickup truck.

"I gotta tell you," he says, "they pulled up in this little freaking rental. The tiniest rental car known to man, and they have basically hollowed out two spots inside to sit in, and the rest of the interior is solid buddy heaters and propane tanks.

"We start pulling shit out, and I'm thinking, 'This is like a clown car! I don't think all this stuff is gonna fit into my truck!'"

It did, of course, so now the generosity of four grateful people in response to the generosity of a team of rescue workers will enable said rescue workers to spend a cold winter generously helping untold people who right now don't even know they're going to need rescuing yet.

At this point, it appears the cycle of blind generosity consuming Western North Carolina is on autopilot. On the day I speak with Jay by phone, he is heading from his home in Georgia back to North Carolina—to help throw a Christmas party for people affected by the storm.

"A lot of these families," he says, "it doesn't look like they're gonna have any kind of Christmas. And we just…well, we're not okay with that."

In the background of our phone connection, I can hear the rumble of Jay's truck, rolling through valleys that two months ago flowed heavy with death and destruction, heading in the direction of some folks he's never met and will most likely never see again. Just to cheer them up a little.

***

It's easy to think of people like Jay—who hurl themselves into service to individuals whose politics are a mystery; whose cultural traditions may be utterly foreign to them—as some sort of benevolent outlier; big-hearted throwbacks in an age when most of us live on isolated islands of selfishness.

But I suggest—and I think Jay and Jackie and Matt & Co. would agree—there is something uniquely generous in the American ethos. Historically, U.S. citizens have been by far the world's most plentiful supplier of foreign humanitarian aid. Even in the economic chaos that came on the heels of COVID-19, individual charitable giving by Americans set new records.

Among industrialized nations not at war, a 2023 study by World Population Review ranked the U.S. squarely as the planet's most charitable country: seventy-six percent of all Americans reported helping a stranger, sixty-one percent donated to a charity, and thirty-eight percent volunteered time to a charitable organization.

Despite the hatred and malevolence we see depicted just about everywhere in the news and on TV; despite the venom that spits from X and comment boards, Americans don't really hate each other. When the rains come and the fires rage; when the markets crash and people are hungry, political and social differences aren't just irrelevant; they're invisible.

We're not that much different from Jay. We're here to help.

Reading the results

Georgetown, Delaware: Return Day

There's No Debate: Everyone Wants a Better Future

Just two weeks ago, the 180-year-old Sussex County Court House had been sitting there decapitated. Its tall, ornate white cupola, removed for restoration six months earlier, rested in an adjacent courtyard, resembling a decorative hat that had been placed on a pew next to its naked-noggined owner.

Braced by scaffolding, the cupola had been attended to by swarming workers replacing rotting wood, repairing broken louvers and re-painting boards crafted from trees felled in the forests that once surrounded Georgetown, a historic Delaware farming community named not for a colonial king, but for the bureaucrat who headed the state commission that created it in 1791.

Now, just in time, a giant crane has given the copula a lift back to where it belongs. From high atop the court house, it presides over a circular town center, the kind Hollywood studios spend millions to recreate: A ring of two-story storefronts and modest government buildings facing a tree-shaded inner circle of public park, punctuated by an ornate concrete fountain.

Were this the summer tourist season, that fountain would be gurgling with water. But now it's November, and the flow has been shut off before the drains can be clogged by a fall of soggy, rust-colored leaves.

Still, the circle is jammed with people, most of them pressed against the south side of the park, cheering and clapping as a prototypical small-town parade passes by. Here comes the Indian River High School band playing "America the Beautiful." Here's the Long Neck Fire Department in their vintage truck, sounding the horn as the driver muscles the enormous horizontal steering wheel. Here's a local family that, for reasons known only to them, decided to dress up like the characters on *SpongeBob SquarePants* and then march in public that way.

And here, to a curiously muted reception, come three men representing the Sons of the Confederacy, one bearing the battle flag of the Army of Northern Virginia.

But most importantly, here comes a caravan of convertibles, each one carrying one or two waving people, sitting up where the rear headrests should be, their feet resting on the seats.

Politicians, of course. Like at every small-town parade in every burgh in America.

But there's a difference: For one thing, they can't be running for anything, because the election was just two days ago. For another, on several of those cars, the now-outdated campaign signs fastened to the doors reveal that these two grinning, glad-handing people were opponents in that election: One Republican and one Democrat.

Standing on the curb, flanked by flag-waving parade enthusiasts, I watch a silver BMW convertible–occupied by two State Senate candidates who just two days ago were desperately hoping for each other's failure—as it rolls past. By looking at their faces, it is impossible to tell who is the winner and who is not. They wave to the crowd; occasionally smile at each other. When an obvious supporter strides into the street to shake hands with one candidate, he gestures to the other and introduces her by name. Both seem, well, *happy*.

My mind reels back to the most recent general election: the name calling, the insults, the unadulterated words of hatred. I think about the spittle-spotted Facebook posts, lobbed like canisters of mustard gas, that frayed friendships and fractured families.

I look at these two, and a part of me wants to cry.

***

"Welcome to Return Day!" bellows a man standing atop a grandstand in front of the court house, his amplified voice reverberating around the circle. "Only in Delaware!"

He's right about that.

You can sniff out every town, county, and state in the Union and you will find nothing like Return Day in Sussex County, Delaware, where on the Thursday after each general election former political opponents ride together to hear the official results of Tuesday's vote.

Some form of Return Day has been held in Georgetown every two years since 1791. In those days of horse and cart travel, and before there were any precinct voting stations, residents of the county had to journey all the way to Georgetown to cast their ballots. Many would return two days later (hence the name "Return Day") to hear the results announced by the town crier, 1791's answer to David Muir, in front of the court house.

Not everyone bothered to leave town, though. Even though Georgetown was centrally located, it was still a twenty-mile journey from the county's most far-flung reaches. Rather than make that difficult round-trip in one day, lots of Southern Delawareans made a week of it, staying in town and engaging in such eighteenth century diversions as attending band concerts, doing some drinking (or lots of drinking) and wagering on cockfights, the post-colonial version of UFC.

After just a few years, the informal street festival that unfolded in Georgetown between Election Day and Results Day was formalized: In 1812, the Thursday after the election was declared Return Day.

In a striking show of patriotism and unreasonably good sportsmanship, all the candidates rode to the square in wagons, the winners facing front and the losers with their backs to the horse.

No one knows how many times the rivals-on-wheels tradition has been broken, but it appears the first notable modern-day breach came in 1990, when then-Senator Joe Biden and that year's opponent, M. Jane Brady, walked the parade route separately instead of riding together. (Eighteen years later, Biden again walked the route alone after his opponent for the vice-presidency, Sarah Palin, didn't show.)

***

Kim Hoey Stevenson

Whether or not all the candidates will, in future years, continue to cozy up with their rivals (and it seems fewer are willing to do that each go-round), in my fever dream of a future where Americans somehow relate to each other as people, and not as parties, it becomes essential that the traditions of Return Day persist. I don't expect to see it replicated in every U.S. town square, but at the very least, I need to know it will survive here.

"Oh, it's a big part of what Delaware is all about," says Kim Hoey Stevenson, one of the two State Senate candidates who chose to ride together this time around. Stevenson, a Republican, came out on the losing side in her race against the Democratic incumbent, Russ Huxtable. But in a gesture that perhaps flies in the face of 21st Century GOP combativeness, Stevenson was the first to suggest they attend Return Day together.

It was on election day 2024—in a national political climate where rival candidates seemed reluctant to breathe the same air—that Stevenson ran into Huxtable at a polling site. She reminded him of his Return Day responsibility, no matter who won.

"I said, 'Russ, I can get us a car—I'm expecting us to ride together,'" she recalls as we sip hot drinks at the busy Notting Hill Coffee Shop in Lewes's main street. "While we were talking, another candidate overheard us and said, 'I didn't think we did that anymore.'"

I have offered Stevenson half of my Ooey Gooey, a chewy, doughy confection encased in enough melted brown sugar to match the annual agricultural output of Cuba, but she waves me off.

Kim Hoey Stevenson & Russ Huxtable

"I'm trying to cut out sugar," she says, and now I feel a bit bad because just sitting near this thing is probably enough to send someone into diabetic shock.

Born and raised in Delaware, Stevenson grew up attending Return Day with her family.

"It was a big deal for us," she recalls. "I wasn't thinking about ever running for office, of course. I was just a kid. But I did know that if I ever got elected to something around here, I would not want to miss Return Day.

"I mean, don't we all long for something like Return Day? Don't we all want to be seen, to be heard, to be loved and respected, whether we win or lose? Those are the basics.

"We want community."

When I catch up with Huxtable, the victor, a few days later, he hastens to assure me he was planning to spend Return Day alongside Stevenson all along.

"I was already working on getting a car—Kim just beat me to it," he says as we drink coffee at the local Panera Bread, where he often meets up with constituents.

"Return Day is the period at the end of the sentence," he says. "You're here with the person you were competing for votes against, and now you're saying 'It's all over.' Elections are supposed to be over. They have an end and you move on. I don't know why some people forget that.

"The fact is, even after one person has won an election and the other person has not, you're still equals. If Kim calls me and has some thoughts to share, I'm gonna listen. Why would I not? We all have a civic voice, whether you're in the Republican Party, the Democratic Party, or the Mandalorian Party."

He waits a beat to read my quizzical face.

"Yes," he says, "we have a Mandalorian Party in Delaware."

As I listen to these two grassroots politicians use words like "community" and "equals," I feel my heart sinking into a sort of hopeless nostalgia—mourning for a time that is so recent it's within the lifespan of your average house cat.

"My campaign slogan was 'People, Not Politics,'" says Stevenson, "and I think that reflects the way our political conversation should be."

She wraps her fingers around her paper coffee cup, raises it to her nose, and softly inhales the mist of minty tea rising above its lip. Her eyes follow the swirling steam. She talks softly of an impossibly magical time when politics was a continuing discussion of preferred methods for attaining common goals.

"I was in France a while back," she says, "and I was watching these children playing; running around, yelling to each other, laughing with each other. I said to their father, 'They play just like kids back in the United States.'

"And he said, 'Of course, Kim. They're all made by the same process.'

"He's right. We're all here through the same process. And we all want and need fresh air, clean water a vibrant economy, good schools.

"We may have different ways of getting there, but really, we're all looking for the same things."

Taking a widescreen look at the political climate, Huxtable says he sees only a handful of issues on which mainstream voters' differences may be intractable.

"The big two would be reproductive rights and some elements—and I must emphasize *some*—on climate," he says. "Other than those, I can't think of any issues that we can't approach in a bipartisan manner."

***

It's early afternoon, but the November sun is already slanting through the trees of Georgetown's Circle when Kirk Lawson, the town's crier since 2014, emerges onto the second-floor courthouse balcony. In his bow tie, vest and silk top hat—inherited from his great-uncle, who was crier during the Kennedy administration—Lawson resembles a Ziegfield Follies chorus boy. He is accompanied by Sheriff Robert Lee—looking very *Doc Holliday* in a wide-brimmed black hat and gray vest—who, in accordance with time-honored tradition, has handed the election results to the crier.

"Hear ye, hear ye," the crier proclaims, holding the official document at arm's length. "At noon time today, the board of canvas of Sussex County met behind me in Superior Court chambers with resident Judge Craig A. Carstens and Associate Justice Mark H. Connor of Superior Court of the State of Delaware, and certified the following election returns…"

What follows is, basically, a reading of the Sussex County Election Day ballot, with the precise number of votes for each candidate. (In a blow to the county's Republican party, which once reigned supreme in this agrarian region, Presidential Candidate Kamala Harris handily beat out the eventual national winner, Donald Trump. The shift is due largely to tens of thousands of retirees moving here from New York, Philadelphia and Washington, DC.)

There are flurries of applause from the crowd for some contests, apparent indifference for others—but by far the most enormous response is for Sussex County Clerk of the Peace Norman "Jay" Jones, Jr., occupant of the position since 2017, who ran unopposed and earned five times the number of votes gained by any other county candidate.

Both major gubernatorial candidates are present, as are the two U.S. Senate hopefuls and those who ran for State Insurance Commissioner. None seem quite as comfortable in the presence of their former rivals as Stevenson and Huxtable, and not all of them rode to the reviewing stand in the same vehicle. But they are here, and, for the most part, the spirit of Return Day is being honored. The town crier's reading is unexpectedly short and, truth be told, a bit anticlimactic after all the lead-up. Surely this is one of the least-demanding municipal jobs on record.

"These are the Sussex County voter tallies from the Department of Elections here in Georgetown," he winds up. "Some may ask why only Sussex County? Today, that's all that matters!"

Return Day could easily end right then and there, with a litany of numbers and a peaceful transition of power. But for reasons lost in the mists of Sussex County's Indian River Bay, Return Day's originators added one last element; one that, in the conflicted twenty-first century, sticks a 180-year-old thumb in the eye of those who thrive on stirring up divisions and smoldering hatred between the nation's political factions. Standing at a podium atop the reviewing stand, the day's master of ceremonies—a fresh-faced young newsman from a local TV station—holds aloft a ceremonial hatchet.

Return Day – Burying the hatchet

Attached to a polished wooden handle, the hatchet is an undersized brass affair, elaborately engraved with a floral pattern and perforated with a heart-shaped hole.

"I have in my hand the hatchet," says the emcee, stating the obvious with an air of momentous import. He gestures toward a wooden box set upon the podium; a dark-stained container held together by finely cut box joints. The wood of the box is largely cut away on each long side to create a schematic scene suggesting a forest clearing. Framed in the carved clearing is the outline of an ax, stuck in a tree stump. Clear sheets of plexiglass line the inside of the box, enabling it to hold a few buckets of sand.

"We will now be burying the hatchet," intones the emcee, "in sand from Lewes Beach."

There's a smattering of applause, possibly from witnesses who hail from the town of Lewes, which lies almost exactly seventeen miles northeast of where we're standing and is the eighteenth century county seat of Sussex.

The first official Return Day, in 1812, unfolded in a very different United States. The country was at war with England, and as the King's red coats swarmed the countryside, it's a safe bet Return Days of that era featured ironclad shows of national unity. But it wouldn't last: The event became especially fraught during the runup to the Civil War, with Delawareans—in a Northern state with pronounced Southern sensibilities — sharply divided in their loyalties. Still, even as brothers and friends set off to fight for opposite causes, Return Day persisted; winners and losers still finding the fortitude to ride in the same carriages.

Post-Civil War, Sussex County's agrarian south remained stubbornly in

Dixie's thrall. Through most of the twentieth century, the area persisted as a Deep South outpost, but that began to change with the 1951 construction of the Delaware Bay Bridge, a twin-spanned engineering marvel that suddenly linked Washington, DC and Annapolis, MD to the Delmarva Peninsula. (The ferry that had provided service across the five-mile-wide bay shut down the day the bridge opened.) Then the state of Delaware widened two-lane Route 1—which had once meandered down the spine of the peninsula from Wilmington, narrowing in small towns and creeping across skinny bridges—into a four-lane highway.

Ocean City, Maryland, exploded as a tourist destination. The formerly sleepy beach town of Rehoboth Beach, Delaware went, in mere decades, from a lazy church camp settlement to staking its claim as "America's Summer Capital."

Newcomers filtered in. Slowly, steadily, the results announced on Return Day began to look more like those in Philadelphia and Baltimore. The long-timers took notice.

In 1969, the population of Sussex County was about 80,000 people. They were almost certainly outnumbered by large farm animals. By 2000, the number was roughly twice that— and since then the population has continued to grow between 2.5 and 3 percent annually. Now, about a quarter-million human beings call the county home. As city folk poured into Sussex County—first to play and then to live—the families who'd owned and farmed the land of southern Delaware for centuries found their attitudes and traditions not just pushed into the shadows, but often virulently ridiculed and resisted.

Even today, there is a palpable melancholy among those who recall coastal Delaware as it was—and who see newcomers as determined to reshape it into something they don't recognize. One guy from Georgetown, who may have missed his calling as a beat poet, put it this way in a post on the social media platform NextDoor: "You came here from there because you didn't like there. Now you want to change here to be like there. If you want here to be like there you should have never left there to come here!"

Summoning up the spirit of Return Day, the recently re-elected Russ Huxtable insists there's every reason to believe the two groups that someone described to me as the "Come Heres" and the "From Heres" can work toward common goals.

"The answer to political dissent is, often, to simply talk with each other," he says.

One clear opportunity for finding consensus, he says, is the issue of affordable housing.

"Just a few years ago, *nobody* wanted affordable housing here," he says. "But we conducted a listening tour, meeting with people to explain if you don't have affordable housing, you won't have anyone here to make the hospitals run; to work in the stores and restaurants.

"And you know what? I don't hear anyone speaking out against affordable housing anymore."

Of course, there's still the debate over just where that housing should go, but that discussion, he says, is still ongoing.

"There's a dialog," he says. "And if we're respectful of one another, we can find the place where we can all get some measure of what we think is best for the community."

***

On the Return Day reviewing stand, local leaders of the Republican, Democratic, and Libertarian parties (no Mandalorians here today) all have a hand on the ceremonial hatchet. Together they set it into the sand-filled box. Some extra sand is poured over it and the lid is closed for two years (It is worth noting that the "Burying the Hatchet" ritual is inspired by a Native American tradition dating back to at least the Iroquois Confederacy).

"I now declare the official end of Campaign 2024 in Sussex County," the emcee says. After handshakes all around, the parties go back to their respective corners.

There is one last matter of business to attend to: Somewhere near downtown, an ox has been roasting all day. It is now to time to slice the poor guy up and distribute free ox roast sandwiches to everyone in attendance.

The line is long and winding.

"Free ox sandwiches!" shouts a man in a white hat, slinging ox like a pioneer short order cook. "Ox free for everyone!"

It's Return Day. And even the ox gets it.

An End or a Beginning

You may be surprised to be entering the final turn so soon—nineteen chapters and we're already at the what-did-we-learn section?

Look, I know your time is valuable. I had other chapters in mind about the universal bonding qualities of things like stargazing, and wine, and babies, and 72-degree days. But really, I think you've got the idea by now: The list of things that bind Americans whether they like it or not is really kind of endless. The list of things that separate us: Not so much.

When I began this project, a part of me hoped that at some point the nation's heated political climate would cool to a point where I'd have to call my editor and say "It was a close one, but thank goodness we won't need this book."

Well, that didn't happen.

As I write this, the factions of America seem to be walking in lockstep in opposite directions to the point where they can hardy even see each other, much less exchange meaningful communiques.

I'm not expecting some kind of political détente. For that to happen, one of the prevailing political factions in the United States would have to make an *en masse* about-face, and I don't know one person who thinks that is ever going to happen.

So what do we have left?

The answer, I suspect, lies in the most pessimistic line of optimism I can imagine: America may well be, as many say, beyond the point of irreconcilable differences—but like divorced spouses who cannot afford to own two houses, we can at least sit on the same couch and watch *Ted Lasso* together at night.

Anyone hoping their cultural clan will one day win the upper hand for good is living in a fool's paradise. No matter who is running the government, as it stands now half the country will feel they are being unfairly dictated to, and the other half will firmly believe they are charting a course that will, in the end, be best for everybody, even those who bitterly oppose them.

The sharp and often bitter dialogue among those factions will, and should, continue, probably indefinitely. And that means, more than ever, all quarters will inevitably need to find ways to not only communicate, but also share their commonalities.

***

In the course of my journeys and conversations for this book, I've come to think of America as an enormous tree with a broad trunk and wide branches reaching out in all directions. Not a two-dimensional thing, like a diagrammed family tree, but a round, impenetrably tangled tree that never looks quite the same from below as you walk around it, your neck craned to make out the details of boughs above.

We are all up there, we Americans, each one of us occupying our own personal stem, connected to a twig, connected to a branch, connected to a trunk, connected to the roots, connected to the earth. Some 350 million stems up there, all catching the breeze just a bit differently, all swaying perpetually out of sync.

Each limb of a tree has its own issues. One side needs more sun. The other could use some shade. A disease might be striking one distant stem; an insect might be chewing at another. Some stems get more water than the others do. Some entire branches, burdened by their own weight, might be in danger of snapping and falling off completely.

But whatever their particular needs—real or imagined—the twigs are all part of the same tree. Crawl off any twig and shimmy down the branches, and you will inevitably reach the broad trunk; the point at which every twig has an undeniably shared interest.

The American Tree has never been a nicely shaped boxwood. For 250 years, the thing has defied all attempts to topiary it to resemble, say – and I'm just spitballing here – an elephant or a donkey. Some of those twigs have been at quiet and not-so-quiet war with each other ever since the tree first pushed its way through the topsoil.

So, perhaps this current, wind-battered growing season is not fundamentally different from the ones that came before. Just maybe, the voices from our information boxes of choice are sounding their shrill alarms not out of patriotic fervor but in a cynical play for our eyes and ears.

Those voices are trying to convince us the American Tree has been split asunder by a lightning bolt; that there is no coming back from the issues and insults that divide us.

I respectfully disagree. In fact, I rather arrogantly suggest there has been no better time for each of us to pull back from our twiggy perches, crawl down along the limbs and find the point where the trunk of the American Tree has not yet diverged into branches; that serendipitous sweet spot where the tree's rings sit in near-perfect concentricity – the core that makes us unmistakably, inseparably American.

***

It all comes down to a theme I encountered at every stop I made in my country-hopping voyage of discovery: Everybody wants to be seen, so why not see them in the best possible light?

What if we were all to one day come to an agreement that, despite our vast differences, we all have one job to do as Americans—and that is to preserve America as a place where people can think and act differently, can disagree bitterly, can choose not to like each other—yet also respect each other's roles in making our society work?

This brings to mind, ironically, a stop in my quest that seemed, on the surface, to contradict the very premise of this book.

While I was in Reno, Nevada, visiting the offices of the Nevada Peer Support Network, I had the privilege to sit down with some remarkable front-line workers; the people we call "heroes" whenever things go south, then promptly forget all about when life is good: soldiers, cops, and health care workers. To a person, they affirmed that among rank-and-file responders and military, politics almost never colors their commitment to mission. Relentless training and personal disposition pretty much conspire to focus their attention on the immediate events surrounding them.

But one after another, they bemoaned in the saddest way how the electronic media—and by that I mean news, commentary, and the web—define who they are and what they stand for, even when those messages are only tangentially related to the truth.

"I'm tired of the puppet show," sighed Anthony Jackson, a former Marine who served four tours in the Middle East, followed by seven deployments as a U.S. Military contractor. You'd think that after all that, Jackson would have the license to define himself and his accomplishments—but instead, upon his return, he found that the "puppet show" of TV news had hijacked his real-life narrative in order to advance the agendas of people he did not even know.

"When you're deployed," Jackson said, "you're dealing with the events of the day. Nothing else really matters. You come back here from overseas, and you see all these talking heads in ties and skirts, supposedly telling your story."

Jackson clears his throat. He has a story.

"This was in Afghanistan, after Obama had spent a year dropping 26,000 bombs in the region. That's, like, three bombs an hour for a year. I was driving with another guy through Kabul, and a street kid came running up to my window. It was dusk, but he could see I was an American.

"The kid was freaking out. He ran alongside our truck for blocks, beating on my window, screaming, throwing his hands up in the air, then pointing down to the ground; some kind of pantomime. The guy with me, a Green Beret, never looked at him, just kept staring straight ahead.

"He later explained to me, 'What he's saying is, we dropped bombs on his family, and now he has no one, and we should pay him for his pain.'

"Of course. We'd bombed the shit out of the place. The kid was all alone."

Jackson returned to the U.S. with stories like that; stark evidence, he believed, that America's war machine was less about liberating oppressed people and more about propping up the weapons industry.

"But when I came back, with first-hand experience, the puppet show people looked at me and said, 'Oh, this is just a symptom of your PTSD.' That was very discouraging."

Too often, he said, people are willing to look no farther than the labels they apply to others.

"We're so proud of our labels," he says. "We divide each other up by our labels. It's like the allegory of Plato's Cave: Everyone's watching the shadows on the wall, and that becomes their reality. The puppet show."

John Mon Père has spent his entire life as a cop—first in Santa Ana, CA, then in Fresno, and now with the force in Truckee.

"Most cops are conservative," says Mon Père. "And I think that gets reinforced in them when they see the kinds of people who are on Welfare, or the people whose homes they are always getting called to. They don't think about, maybe, what social situations led to those conditions."

In other words, he said, conservative cops tend to interpret crime and poverty conditions in terms that echo the narrative from conservative media.

But then again, he added, more liberal people are taking their cues from their preferred media outlets, as well.

"Look at NPR (National Public Radio)," he says. "They assume police—all police—are racists. Anytime a person of color dies in custody, it's because of race. Well, that's just horse shit.

"The fact is, I've always preferred working in communities of color."

The power of media to overrule personal experience was driven home to Denise Mon Père, John's niece and a Veteran's Administration nurse in Fresno.

"The one time politics came up among the people who work with me at the VA was during COVID-19," she says. "There were employees in the

ICU, including a good friend of mine, who questioned COVID treatments; questioned government regulations on the treatments. They were super anti-vaccine. And they were in health care, with people dying of COVID. It was mind-boggling.

"I still don't understand it, but I do know the media they chose to consume played a huge, huge role in that."

So, Bill, I hear you saying, why are you, this late in the game, presenting us with examples of ways Americans not only don't see eye-to-eye, but may in fact be at each other's throats?

In every case cited above, the essential problem can be boiled down to: People very seldom label themselves; labels are most often imposed upon them by people who don't want to think too deeply (libtard, Nazi, hater, etc.). Everyone deserves to be seen and heard on their own terms, and accepted for who they are, whether their personal values and characteristics resonate with us or not. I don't just happen to believe the majority of Americans have enough self-awareness, and a big enough heart, to do just that—there is ample evidence that, under a galaxy of conditions, they prove themselves capable daily.

If you were to seek out my Facebook page, you'd see that my own political outlook is nothing less than strident. I am as guilty as most of lobbing occasional mortars of contempt at the philosophies that I'm convinced may lead to the ruin of the country I grew up in. I try not to initiate unpleasantness—but to be honest, when attacked, the writer in me at times cannot resist weaving elaborately literate rejoinders of which, I like to think, Cyrano himself would be proud.

I'm giving myself a pass there. That's the social media battleground we all occupy, and to cede it to those with whom we disagree would be to let the most egregious slanders against what I see as truth and justice go unchallenged.

But one thing I never, ever do is sign off with a one-word insult. Scroll through any political message board and you'll see those cowardly cutoffs: "Libtard." "Nazi." "Idiot." "Traitor." As for me, I don't settle down for a social media tête-a-tête without determining that I will counter each and every argument coolly and methodically until my opposite number either grows weary (most of the time) or acknowledges my point (never).

"Why do you bother?" a digital observer once interjected.

"Because truth telling takes time," I answered.

One thing my debate opponents will never say of me: "He didn't hear my side."

I'm reminded of the words my friend Alison Pratte, the therapist, said as we parted ways back in Sparks, Nevada: "Sometimes I think all the United States needs is a good marriage counselor."

Taking Alison's words to heart, I tracked down an actual psychiatrist and psychoanalyst who, as it turns out, agrees.

"I've been doing this for fifty years," says Dr. Alice Maher, whose practice is in Manhattan. "The first forty years, nobody talked about politics. The last ten years, everybody talks about politics. It's like we're all in the same shared trauma."

There's nothing new, Maher says, in holding opposing attitudes toward someone you know—and even someone you love.

"My whole career is about tolerating paradox and ambiguity and conscious and unconscious," she says. "You know: I can consciously love you and my unconscious can hate you. That's human nature."

Prior to, oh, let's say, the arrival of a national politician for whom unvarnished insults are the coin of their realm, Maher says, most people kept the quiet part quiet and only expressed the out-loud part. But norms have changed, partly due to public example, largely thanks to social media technology that spares us the inconvenience of having to witness the hurt feelings or blind anger our harsh words inspire.

"The first step in couples therapy is to listen to the other person and then repeat back what they're saying. Then you can argue; then you can share your side.

"We need to do that with our political differences, too. Otherwise, if we perceive the presence of someone who thinks differently as a threat, we do this fight or flight thing.

"We delete them. We ghost them. We block them. We unfriend them. Or we have a knockdown, drag-out fight. What we can't do is listen, because it's too threatening to listen."

Maher is founder and president of Waging Dialogue, a program dedicated to developing the emergence of effective communications across interpersonal and intergroup divides.

"Political, scientific, and moral arguments don't work," Maher states in Waging Dialogue's online manifesto. "Calling out and canceling don't work…We prejudge each other and quickly find others who agree with our distortions."

Maher is calling for nothing less than a large-scale social movement "to stop mocking, accusing, blocking, canceling, and unfriending people who see the world differently from the way we do; a movement to find new ways to communicate effectively across vast human divides."

For now, Maher is enlisting fellow mental health professionals to infuse their work with the animating concepts of Waging Dialogue. She is working with Braver Angels, the nationwide group that seeks to find common dialogue among Republicans, Democrats and Independents, to devise effective and scalable parliamentary-style debates.

And in what can be seen as a don't-beat-'em, join-'em strategy, Maher is shopping around a smartphone app that will use an algorithm to match subscribers of one political persuasion with those of another, fostering a decidedly convivial discussion forum that might be described as the Anti-X.

I don't need to tell you—or Maher—she is pushing this heavy, square-wheeled cart uphill.

"Relating to people who are different from you takes practice," she says. "You can't just will yourself to do it. It's hard work, and you have to listen, and make mistakes, and correct your errors, and tolerate the discomfort and go back for more.

"Everyone prefers life to be like sporting matches: my Mets versus your Yankees. But that's because if you love the Mets, you never really need to get to know those Yankees."

***

The central theme of this book is perfectly reflected in the responses that will inevitably greet its publication: In person, people will clasp my arm and enthuse that this is exactly the book America needs right now. On social media, anonymous posters will from a distance flame its naïve, almost childish optimism; ridicule its simplistic approach to the issues that divide us.

In short: If this country's society is going to survive, it will happen not on our computer screens but in the face-to-face encounters that define our humanity.

Either that, or our society will die on a hill of mean Tweets, ripped to shreds by the shrapnel of anonymous, faceless, digital firebombers.

***

So here comes the end of the book, the part where I learn a lesson, and I think it's a difficult one. I feel compelled to return to that Facebook feud with the guy I've known since I was a teenager; the guy who questioned my very spirituality just because I didn't vote for the same candidate he did.

I cut him off. Couldn't take it anymore. Said I loved him, sure, but snipped the cord of connection, nevertheless.

Here in Delaware, we have what I contend are some of the most beautiful sunsets God has endowed Earth with. Why don't I just head out to the back porch tonight and snap a photo of one and send it to him? No words, no emojis. Just a shared sunset.

Better idea: Why don't we all do that? Doesn't have to be a sunset. A picture of your dog, a link to your favorite song, a poignant article about a charity.

Or, better yet, a photo of the two of you together. Long ago. Before the world whispered in your ear that disagreement = death.

I am reminded of a notification that often appears on my computer screen:

Connection Lost. Reconnecting.

Acknowledgments

You don't want to go to the movies with me. Like a die-hard baseball fan who stays until the final out in a 15-3 shellacking, I remain riveted to my theater seat until the final copyright notification rolls by at the end of the credits (You'd be surprised how often the same studio grip's name appears. And aren't you as curious as I am as to who the intimacy coordinator was for that red-hot love scene?).

What we've got going here right now is my book's version of the end credits: The part where I express my heartfelt thanks to all the people who helped make this little tome possible. Do me a favor: Stick around. These folks—along with those I'm somehow forgetting—deserve it.

First of all, if not for all the astonishingly generous people who appear in these pages, this book would have been a work of fiction. My unbound thanks to you all. I sincerely wish I could afford to present you all with comp copies, but that is no way to run a business.

Believe it or not, I did not happen to already know one-hundred or so people around the country whose political positions aligned with each chapter's topic. I do, however, have a nationwide network of old friends and new acquaintances who not only suggested possible interview subjects, but who also took it upon themselves to introduce me to them. In particular, a big, gold, imaginary MVP Trophy goes to one of my oldest friends, Alison Pratte in Reno, Nevada, and one of my newest, Mike Kent of Traverse City Tourism, for seeking out political figures of opposing camps who, miraculously in a time like this, not only get along, but actually like each other.

Many of the travels documented in this book were piggybacked on assignments for outlets to which I frequently contribute, including *National Geographic, The Saturday Evening Post*, and *Delaware Beach Life*. In addition, some vignettes included in these pages first appeared, in significantly different form and context, within articles I wrote for those same publications. My thanks, especially, to *AARP Bulletin* for their blessing as I drew heavily on my account of an earlier visit to Madrid, New Mexico. Also, to Terry Plowman, publisher and editor of *Delaware Beach Life*, for letting me largely lift my chapter on Delaware hunters from his pages.

I still can't believe my good luck in stumbling across the big-hearted people at Builders Movement, without whom two pivotal chapters of this book—those on abortion and guns—would never have happened. Tori Larned was my constant contact with Builders, and I owe her big time. Keep an eye out for Builders projects in your community, or better yet visit their website at BuildersMovement.org.

Likewise, Susan Glisson, founder of Welcome Table, not only spoke with me at length; she also pointed me in the direction of the Family Circle project at Arlington House. Welcome Table provides mediation services for private and public groups nationwide (WelcomeTableCollaborative.org).

It had not occurred to me to include a chapter about Alberta, Canada, until I was invited to visit Calgary, Banff and Jasper by the extremely hospitable people at Pursuit Collection, owners of the Pyramid Lake Lodge. Thank you, Rose Chase, for thinking of me.

I was writing a travel story about Colorado Springs when my hosts, The Hotel Polaris at the U.S. Air Force Academy, were kind enough to let me stay on for a few extra days researching the bipartisan efforts to preserve trails in the Rocky Mountains. Thanks to Kristin Yantis of Malon Yantis Public Relations for making that happen.

There are times when a writer really, really wishes he could have included a particular interview, but for reasons of structure or (relative) brevity it just can't happen. I had not even heard of the sinking town of Willcox, Arizona until I shared a delightful coffee one Tucson morning with Nico Lorenzen, the conservation and wildlife associate for Wild Arizona, who is a font of knowledge regarding Sonoran Desert ecology. Thanks for the talk and the tip, Nico.

This paragraph is about Debbie Geiger, owner of Geiger & Associates in Tallahassee, Florida, who has, on press trips from coast to coast, shuttled me and a legion of other travel writers from airports to hotels to wineries to windswept mountaintops, always with the greatest of humor, always spouting so much inside local information you'd swear she'd been born in, say, Door County, Wisconsin, rather than sunny Florida. It was Debbie who introduced me to the musical wonders of Muscle Shoals, Alabama. She also got me backstage at the Grand Ole Opry. It was Debbie who invited me to Brenham, Texas, where I finally began to understand the oddball ins and outs of the Lone Star State. Thanks, Debbie. Save me a seat in the minivan.

Now for the more cosmic thank-yous: First of all, to the impressive, inimitable Robert Mrazek, my resourceful publisher, sharp-eyed editor and boundless friend, who toiled for years to figure out a project that fit our particular dynamic. Sorry the resurrected Elvis screenplay didn't work out, Bob, and thanks for going to bat for my doomed novel about the *National*

Enquirer writer who uncovers a terrorist plot involving exploding VCRs but no one will believe him because he's a *National Enquirer* writer. It was worth the wait.

James Bock, you had two jobs: Edit my book and get to know your newborn child. I admire your work/home balance, and especially your unique skill for repeatedly spotting the repeated words I always repeat.

An alternate dedication that I toyed with for this book was "To my children, left and right, centered in love." It's no glib turn of a phrase: As I say elsewhere in this book, among my proudest accomplishments is having raised kids who think for themselves. I suppose most of the credit should go to the woman who was home with them all day, their mother and my late wife, Cindy Kanaley Newcott. Anyone who knew Cindy will tell you there was no one more stridently outspoken in her beliefs and political positions, but she also had an unbound sense of love and respect even for those whose lifestyles and social stances were polar opposites of hers. That generous spirit could not help but rub off on our children, and I will be forever thankful to her for that.

Finally, my most profound thanks and fathomless love to Carolyn Kent Newcott, who from the moment she married me in 2011 (and even before) had a simple list of demands: That I always follow my creative impulses, that I never fail to seize opportunities for new experiences, and that I treasure the joy in every moment I'm privileged to walk this planet. With Carolyn in my life, that last pursuit is automatic.

In 2012, Carolyn voted for Barack Obama. I voted for Mitt Romney. We each still think we got that one right. But as I hope I've demonstrated on these pages, there is so, so much more to life – and love – than politics.

About the Author

Bill Newcott is the weekly film critic and frequent travel writer for *The Saturday Evening Post*. Earlier, he was Senior Editor and an award-winning Space Science and Expeditions Editor at *National Geographic* magazine. During seventeen years at *AARP the Magazine,* where he also served as Senior Editor, he received the Lowell Thomas Award for best travel coverage and created AARP's Movies for Grownups franchise. His Gracie Award-winning "AARP Movies for Grownups Radio Show" aired weekly for twelve years.

Bill is the author of *All the Right Wrong Turns: True (And Sometimes Twisted) Tales of Coastal Delaware from the Back Roads to the Beaches* (2021) and its sequel, *More Right Wrong Turns* (2024), both honored by the National Federation of Press Women. He also contributed a chapter to the *National Geographic Explorations Atlas* (2000). And in what seems like another life, from 1980 to 1990, he was a writer for *The National Enquirer* in Lantana, Florida. He never met a space alien.

Bill lives in Lewes, Delaware, with his wife, Carolyn.

Many thanks to you, the readers of,

DIVIDED WE STAND

FOLLOW ME ON

FACEBOOK:

www.facebook.com/BillNewcottTravel
www.facebook.com/MoviesForTheRestOfUs

AND

INSTAGRAM: www.instagram.com/billnewcott/

CHECK OUT MY WEBSITE:

www.billnewcott.com

CHECK OUT MY WEEKLY ARTICLES ONLINE AT THE SATURDAY EVENING POST

www.saturdayeveningpost.com/author/b-newcott/

TO SCHEDULE BOOKSTORE, LIBRARY OR BOOK CLUB EVENTS

Email: wnewcott@gmail.com

www.ingramcontent.com/pod-product-compliance
Lightning Source LLC
LaVergne TN
LVHW052353100826
845147LV00013B/826
9798994195833